THEATRE CAFE
PLAYS ONE

COMPANY OF ANGELS

Company of Angels fosters and produces innovative theatre for young audiences.

Following the success of *Hannah & Hanna*, *Club Asylum* and *Crime and Punishment in Dalston*, Company of Angels' latest productions have firmly established the company's reputation for challenging, high-quality work: *Virgins* (in co-production with The Junction, Cambridge, Edinburgh Festival 2006 and national tour), *RISK* (Spring 2007 in collaboration with macrobert arts centre, Stirling, Y Dance and The Tron Theatre, Glasgow) and *Truckstop* (co-produced with Eastern Angels, Stage Award Edinburgh Festival 2007, national and Eastern region tour) were all very well received by critics and audiences alike.

Company of Angels also actively nurtures and supports emerging artists through the *Young Angels* programmes and the *Angels Associates* scheme.

The company not only produces shows but also initiates innovative projects and new models of work. *Theatre Café* (2004), *Theatre Café Europe* (2007) and our *Young Europe* (2004) season have successfully brought new foreign plays to UK audiences; *Asylum Seeker Narratives* and its successor *Project R* are community schemes that directly involve young people; and the *GAP Theatre Project*, a unique peer-mentoring initiative, is currently being expanded having finished its third successful run in 2007.

Projects currently underway include: *Theatre Café Festival* (November 2008) a new festival merging the company's work with emerging artists and our practice of both promoting and producing new international plays in the UK; the British premiere of *Invasion!* by award-winning Swedish writer Jonas Hassen Khemiri in co-production with The Junction, Cambridge and Soho Theatre (early 2009); and the Gap Theatre Project Teacher Training (summer and autumn 2008).

Artistic Director: John Retallack
Producer/Dramaturge: Teresa Ariosto
General Manager: Vanessa Fagan/Virginia Leaver (job-share)
Finance Manger: David Harris
Contact: www.companyofangels.co.uk
      126 Cornwall Road, London SE1 8TQ
      020 79282811
      info@companyofangels.co.uk

Theatre Café
PLAYS ONE

JONAS HASSEN KHEMIRI
Invasion!
Translated by Frank Perry

JOËL POMMERAT
This Child
Translated by Nigel Gearing

LUTZ HÜBNER
Respect
Translated by Zoë Svendsen

OBERON BOOKS
LONDON

This anthology published in the UK in 2008 by Oberon Books Ltd
521 Caledonian Road, London N7 9RH
Tel: 020 7607 3637 / Fax: 020 7607 3629
e-mail: info@oberonbooks.com
www.oberonbooks.com

A catalogue record for this book is available from the British
Library.

ISBN: 978-1-84002-893-5

Cover artwork by Olivier Wiame

Printed in Great Britain by CPI Antony Rowe, Chippenham.

Contents

Introduction

THEATRE CAFE

Theatre Café is about giving a platform to brilliant new European plays that have had considerable success in their own countries – but which have not been seen in the UK. Company of Angels have now commissioned twelve new translations of plays (including the three in this volume) that have received their first readings at Theatre Café.

Some of the plays have been written expressly for young people, some – like *This Child* – have simply caught the imagination of young people in their own countries.

What is Theatre Café?

Theatre Café is a theatrical space designed to create an informal, intimate atmosphere where audiences can relax and feel very close to a play. Every performance is followed by a discussion – often with the participating presence of the playwright. There's room for audience involvement and also for the writers to benefit from the process.

Theatre Café started in 2004 at the Arcola Theatre in Hackney.

Twelve plays from nine European countries were read over two weeks in the special Theatre Café setting created by designer Liz Cooke.

The twelve plays were selected from among more than 150 submitted; none had been produced in the UK before and three were given their first English translations, commissioned especially for Theatre Café.

The feedback suggests that we succeeded in creating the informal and intimate atmosphere that we wanted. Audiences were unanimous in saying that the scripts in the actors' hands were soon forgotten as they were drawn into the story, while the vast majority of teenagers expressed their liking of the setting and of the possibility for talking informally with actors, writers and directors after the show.

Ten of the twelve authors came over to take part in the event and in the debate. They were enthused by the possibilities offered by Theatre Café.

I didn't know what to expect from a staged reading but I must say that the Theatre Café performance went far beyond what I dared to hope for. The setting itself made a very good connection between audience and actors, and the play worked perfectly in this atmosphere even though it is written for smoke, flying characters and a revolving stage. I kind of forgot it was a staged reading; the papers in their hands became something like a concept rather than a reminder of words or text.
Andri Snær Magnason (Iceland)

The simple set left space for imagination and many things were actually more effective in the reading than they would have been in a full production
Juha Jokela (Finland)

Company of Angels looks for European plays that are original in both form and style and with important stories to tell; they must also be plays that we believe speak to a wider public, beyond the immediate country of origin.

Following the success of the 2004 edition, Theatre Café went to a new level in 2007 with four major events going on simultaneously in four different parts of Europe – in London, in Tallinn, in Lille and in Amsterdam.

Company of Angels collaborated with VAT Teater (Estonia), MUZ Theater (Holland) and Le Grand Bleu (France) and together mounted staged readings of 20 new plays from all over Europe. All of the plays were heard for the first time in each respective language. Company of Angels installed Theatre Café at the Unicorn Theatre and, for the first time, we hosted an international symposium.

After the Symposium, the Swedish Embassy invited Company of Angels to curate a special version of Theatre Café, in order to bring the most original and thought-provoking work being written in Sweden today to the attention of British producers.

We have now succeeded in finding plays that British repertory theatres actually want to produce as a result of seeing them at Theatre Café. The three plays in this anthology are all lined up for production in 2009/10. Company of Angels is actively involved in all of these productions, sometimes in an advisory capacity, in others as a co-producer.

I got some very positive feedback from directors. One of them wants to stage my play in Berlin, at the English Theatre. There are also requests from London. And just the other day the French translator for the Lille reading wrote that it went very well in France and asked if he can send it out to directors and publishing houses over there. This means Theatre Café Europe works and plays circulate, which is always a great thing. I hope the project continues in the following years because there aren't so many like it.
Stefan Peca (Romania)

Theatre Café 2008 has evolved as a festival, taking place in two different London venues, Unicorn Theatre and Southwark Playhouse; it also links the company's current work with emerging artists to its established European dimension.

This year we launched our *Angels Associates* scheme and we currently have eleven young theatre-makers attached to the company; eight of them are directors and there is also a writer, an actor/musician and a movement specialist.

We have two young artists schemes currently on the go and the results of some of this work will be presented at Theatre Café; Mia Theil Have and Max Webster direct Sandholm by Anna Bro, Philip Thorne and Oystein Brager of Imploding Fictions present *Norway Today* by Igor Bauersima – and we see the final presentations by young directors to win the coveted £20,000 Young Angels Theatremakers Award (in collaboration with The Junction in Cambridge) to direct *Invasion!* by Jonas Hassen Khemiri at Soho Theatre in Spring 2009.

Theatre Café Festival is unique because it brings European work and young theatremakers together and shares this with representatives from all over the British theatre industry and beyond.

A lot of interested people are coming together at Theatre Café in 2008; we hope that it will grow annually until by 2011 it becomes an indispensable way of moving plays and artists between different cultures and languages.

Teresa Ariosto and John Retallack
Theatre Café Curators

INVASION!

by Jonas Hassen Khemiri
Translated by Frank Perry

Further Copyright Information

Characters

FOUR ACTORS

A   Man, 40-50 years of age –
Actor 1, Lance, Guide, The Journalist, The Apple-Picker.

B   Man, 20-25 years old –
Arvind, Expert 1, The Fanon Fan plus others.

C   Woman, 25-30 years old –
Actor 2, Lara, Expert 2, Interpreter.

D   Man, 20-25 years old –
Yousef, Expert 3, African Beads Woman, Little Brother.

*The play consists of four monologue sections about the 'fictional'
Abulkasem and three interludes in which a panel of experts
present their analyses/findings concerning the 'real' Abulkasem.
Riddle: who are the real figures hiding behind the names of the
experts?*

IN THE FOYER

*Yousef (**D**) and Arvind (**B**) come into the theatre foyer from the street, dressed in baseball caps and track-suit bottoms. They are each holding a McDonalds straw and some paper napkins; they blow chewed-up bits of paper at each other. They knock one another into members of the audience; they look threateningly at anyone who answers back. They walk round the foyer, making a lot of noise, putting the moves on the odd girl.* (Ey, baby, you are so fine, come and sit with us, we know the guy what wrote the play, we've got VIP-seats, yo baby.)

1 SCENE 1 'ALMQVIST AND ABULKASEM AS A NEW WORD'

*The audience enters. **B** and **D** are sitting next to each other, close to the stage.*

***A** and **C** perform a scene from Carl Jonas Love Almqvist's* Signora Luna. *Highly theatrical tone. **B** and **D** giggle, spoiling the solemnity of the performance.*

A (ACTOR 1): One summer fine, Don Silvio Luna sailed with his consort
And their fair daughter from the mainland of Italy
For the sloping hillsides of the island of Sardinia,
Where, as in chivalric splendour, of his many castles
One was set to gaze wide over the Mediterranean sea;
The city of Cagliari lying not far away and, here,
Wreathed round with holly and olive-trees, the towers
Of Luna's citadel climbed loftily toward the sky.

The sound of wind and ominous-sounding strings.

***B** gets up and pretends to conduct. **B** and **D** take out their drinking-straws and start peppering the stage with wads of paper.*

C (ACTOR 2): That same summer an Arab corsair was driven by the winds
Many leagues from his African homeland towards the North.
Seeking treasure, he cast his anchor by Sardinia's strand
Ashore he went and there Donna Antonia caught his eye.

B makes farting sounds, B and D laugh.

A: Not with violence did he take his lass; the heat of his desire
Bid him lie to for three whole days along that rocky coast.
Never before had his flag failed to flutter for so long!
And yet one more day did he stay there with ship and crew:

C: He captured the shimmering heart of his joyous maiden
But not her mother's approbation, nor her father's favour.
Still the soil of Italy remembers the Arab's name. From the
Northwest of Africa he came, from the tribes of the Mahgreb
Abulkasem by name...

A: The dread pirate captain, who put
The islands of Italy to the torch, that same man?

C: (*Nodding.*) ABULKASEM ALI MOHARREM

A: On the eve of the fourth day, he sailed his ship away,
And with him went Antonia Luna of her own free will.
From the Arab's treasures she bedecked her hair and arms
With pearls, stolen from the tresses of fair Christian ladies.
Two years later – for in haste, though shrouded in darkness,
Must this story move – two years later then...
Abulkasem's frigate hove to in the harbour of Corfu,
A Grecian island to the east of Amalfi town.
For it was then we were at war with the Arabs all
Over the rulership of Sicily – and well I remember it
From my own boyhood – and oh! the battles we lost and won.
But Abulkasem, wounded sore, was forced to retire...

B makes a loud farting sound, A and C lose their thread.

C: (*To B.*) Could everyone just please show X [*The actor's name.*] a little respect...

B: Ey, you're the one should be showing some respect, yo.

A: If you can't behave with common decency, there's really no point in our…

D: Common? Like you're so common. Common that's us!

A loses patience, he starts quarrelling with B and D, who have rushed up onto the stage. Then A starts squabbling with C. They leave the stage, which has been taken over by B and D.

B (ARVIND):   (*Having found a megaphone, he starts shouting through it.*) 'We regret to inform you that Richard, Six B's teacher, is a real slag and drags around a cock the size of a squirrel's and…'

The megaphone stops working. B turns to the audience instead.

One two, one two, are there any real niggas in da house? Any righteous brothers or are you lot just a load of theatrical slags? Uh uh uhn… Who's running the show now then, you ho's? Who's the Shakespeare? Who's Shakespeare now then, bitches?

D (KALIL):   (*To the audience.*) So who's Shakespeare now then, bitches. Who, right? And to that old slag in the entrance what was like (*He imitates her accent.*) 'So all of Hackney's here tonight then, darling' when you saw us, don't go thinking we didn't hear you!

B: 'Izzakly, and – nudge, nudge – your fur coat isn't hanging in the cloakroom any more…'

D: 'Izzakly. Nudge, nudge… Your fur coat isn't hanging in the cloakroom any more, it's for treading on down the toilets, yo!'

Short pause.

B: (*To the audience; without a perceptible accent.*) That's how it all begins. We're at the theatre with our class. This is the first play I've ever seen in my entire life. And it is totally fucked up…

A returns onstage.

A: (*In an exaggeratedly theatrical voice.*)
       One summer fine, Don Silvio Luna sailed with his consort
       And their fair daughter from the mainland of Italy

B: So then I start with that nang farting-trick of mine and they
       all piss themselves, Kalil like most of all. The play gets
       stopped, the actors leave the stage and we fuck around
       while Richard, our teacher, starts shouting…

D: Oh no, no no NO!

B: Bit later the security turns up and we get dumped onto
       the street and one of the bouncers gives Kalil a right going
       over…

       D claps his hands together very loudly.

B: Only we fight back and Chas snap-kicks one of the
       bouncers in the knee and Kalil rips off his identity badge
       and the last thing we hear before we run like fuck for the
       tube is Richard's voice shouting something like…

D: (*Imploringly.*) 'See you tomorrow!'

B: That was the last time we saw Richard… The next day
       there we all were waiting for him in the classroom and he
       never shows… He'd resigned…he'd cracked up, like all the
       others…actually we were feeling a bit ashamed by then
       only no one wanted to admit it, so we rolled down to the
       pool room and played cards instead… Yousef was the first
       bloke to mention the play…

D (YOUSEF): 'Ey, that play last night… Senora Luna by Almqvist.
       You gotta admit it was mad *wack*!'

B: And everyone's like sure. Course it was…

D: 'I mean it, admit it was seriously fucked up!'

B: Sure.

D: 'Come on, bruv, admit it sucked elephant balls'

B: All right, so it was pretty bad, we know…

D: 'Right then, it was so sucky it was…'

B: Ey! We know, so? That's it… And that's when this weird
        thing happens I'll never forget. I've got this awesome
        memory of Yousef just sitting there, a Christian Lebanese
        about this high with this total forest of a moustache, holding
        his cards like some fucking fan. And then he says with this
        kind of embarrassed look on his face,

D: 'Only you gotta admit Abulkasem is a heavy name.'

B: And he really did say it that way…

D: 'Hehveee nayme'.

B: And everyone in the pool hall just stops talking and then…

D AND B: (*Laughing.*) OOOOOOOH!

B: We just laugh and call him a right theatre ponce and Kalil
        says Yousef's Mum gets visited by Abulkasem every night
        and Yousef just…

D: 'No, I just mean, what I mean is, his name like, I've got this
        uncle in Lebanon called Abulkasem…'

        Stream of memories begins.

A: I'm too sexy for your land too sexy for your land

        New York and also France…

D: My uncle Abulkasem!

        A as LANCE starts prancing about.

        Abulkasem was Mum's youngest brother…

A: Lance! My name is Lance for Christ's sake…

D: Sorry. Lance. (*A continues prancing.*) Lance was the official
        stage-name he used here in Sweden. His dream was to be
        a dancer… There was this one problem though – we were
        the only ones who had any idea about Lance's dreams. In
        the day-to-day world he was still called Abulkasem and
        lived in Lebanon where his neighbours used to whisper
        behind his back about his lack of any apparent interest
        in getting married. He worked as some kind of termite
        exterminator…all day he'd wander around the suburbs
        of Beirut with a canister on his back spraying vermin to

death…just to save up enough dosh to come and spend Christmas with us.

The stream of memories ends.

D: 'Nah listen, all I mean is, I just mean his name like, I've got an uncle in Lebanon called Abulkasem…who's like this nang Mafioso…and that's like why I…'

B: And we just pipe down a bit and then…

D AND B: (*Laughing.*) OOOOOOH!

Brief pause.

B: And from that day on Abulkasem sort of became an expression in our class…

D: 'Only you gotta admit Abulkasem is a heavy name…'

B: Soon became…

'Gotta admit Abulkasem is heavy.'

B: Which soon became…

D: 'Gotta admit Abulkasem.'

B: It turned into something we started saying, mostly as a joke at first but then more seriously… In the breaks we'd play pool or sit the corridors like, sharing banana skids and talking about some phat Fresh Prince episode and then someone might say…

D: 'Admit Abulkasem…'

B: And everyone started busting up 'cos…I dunno why… It was just so fucking funny. And soon Abulkasem was like a real word. To start with it meant something was wack like, shabby, shitty, twisted… 'Ey, bruv, how was that party at the weekend?'

D: 'My life, man, it was Abulkasem… No ho's, just a load of white boys, we nicked some videos and split early.'

B: Then, a few weeks later, without my really understanding how…the word changed meaning and started to mean something that was nang, phat, mad good…

D: 'Ey, check out that chick…She is fine, yo, she is slim fit, she is flo-jo, she is mad Abulkasem, admit it…'

B: And later on that same term, like some time in December, when we'd got a replacement for Richard and Kalil had been expelled after (*Pause.*) a bit of bother with the woodwork teacher, Abulkasem came to mean anything at all. It could be an adjective…

D: (*Yawning.*) 'Shit, I'm fucked up Abulkasem, I was up all night checking out films…'

B: A verb…

D: (*In irritation.*) 'Come on Louie, Abulkasem someone else, I didn't have time to do any studying…'

B: It could be an insult…

D: (*Menacingly.*) 'Don't play the Abulkasem, bruv, gimme the cue, it's my turn,'

B: It could be a compliment…

D: (*Happily.*) 'On my mother's life, he was wicked Abulkasem, he scored 14 points in the first quarter.'

B: It became the perfect word… Now and then of course there would be a misunderstanding…

D: 'What d'ya mean, Abulkasem? (*Angrily.*) Oh I get it, okay, you mean Abulkasem? (*Apologetically.*) Right, my bad…'

B: Only usually you'd get it from the context. That's the way it mostly was then… Words kept changing and evolving all the time… Only the strange thing was that a load of other words, like knatch or flous or shooli or krisp were the sort that got overused and then they disappeared… Everyone said them for a month or so and then one day they were just…

D: 'What d'ya say? You still calling flous krisp? Nigga please, that is like so old!'

B: What was odd about Abulkasem was that the word stayed on, it changed, grew and survived…

Brief pause.

Secondary school gave way to sixth-form college, the old gang from school split up, Yousef moved away from the city to study dentistry, we lost Kalil to drugs. I started working as a telemarketing salesman and Chas's the only one I'm still in touch with… We meet up every now and then… Go down town, have a few beers, talk memories, update each other on what's been happening to the old homies. And one evening we were meeting in this bar up West, one of your usual like really chilled places, not super luxurious but chilled all the same, you know…cosy like… So we're standing there just chatting when I suddenly catch sight of her…

D (CHAS): Wassup?

B: Check that out…check it out…

C comes on stage.

D: What?

B: You blind? Check out that babe… Check out the sister! Hot damn!

D: What her? The posh girl dressed all grunge-like? Oh leave it alone, for fuck's sake…

B: You blind or something? Shit, she is so fine, yo. (*To the audience.*) She just walks in off the street and she's alone and… I dunno… How can you describe someone like her? Maybe if I'd been Will Smith I would have rolled right on over and just…

D: (*Dark voice.*) You baby yo baby yo baby YO! You must be tired 'cos you've been running around my brain all day…

B: Then again maybe if I'd been a Brazilian I would have crept up to her and whispered…

D: (*Very breathily.*) I think you are being very beautiful, I want you come home with me.

B: And maybe if I'd been a white boy I'd have backed fourteen beers and just…

D: (*Inaudible slurred hooligan speech.*)

B: She's just so fine. Dark curly hair and awesome sexy lips
      and a cute kind of turned-up nose and the kind of style that
      just screams UPPER CLASS...This ain't no hoodrat, this is
      the real McCoy, top of the range, you know, the kind of girl
      who goes to college, with parents that own their own home
      and drive a BMW, you can bet your life she's got a monthly
      Oystercard and belongs to a gym only she hardly ever goes
      and she hangs out in the Alps during the holidays and HOT
      DAMN, she is so fine! Kapow! Hubbabubba!... Grr! (*Sound
      of sirens!*)

      Panting sounds.

D: So go and chat her up then...

B: Nah... Leave off, bruv, that's not really my scene, you know.

D: Oh come on Arvind... Give it a go, man, don't play the
      fucking Abulkasem. Just go on over to her.

B: She moves to the bar and just then, as if by chance, my
      beer runs out...

      He glugs his beer down in desperation.

      I get up with my knees knocking and dry my sweating
      hands on the thighs of my jeans. And there she is. I get
      close to her, raise my empty bottle to her and smile my
      magic smile...

      In a shaky, teenage voice with a stammer.

      W-w-what's up?

      C ignores him.

B: Wow... I swear she's almost better close up... Not too
      much make-up, black woollen top, worn jeans, sexy black
      boots... So fine... And even though she's playing a bit hard-
      to-get, I can tell there's something special between us...
      Just got to do this right... Calm and steady, block out the
      nerves... Control my voice and then...

      In a shaky, teenage voice with a stammer.

      'Ahuh... So what's your name?'

C: What?

B: So w-w-what's your n-name then?'

C (LARA): (*Bored stiff.*) Lara… What's yours?

B: And I just 'uh-oh – fire! fire! – someone here is hot to trot'
        you know… And I… I'm just about to say my name when I
        catch sight of Chas over there at the table and he gives me
        this thumbs up just like some fucking hitchhiker…

D raises his thumb and leaves the stage.

B: I'm just about to say my name… I don't know why exactly
        but I just can't bring myself to say Arvind… I've always
        hated it… Shit you wouldn't believe how much grief it's
        given me. Everyone's like… 'What's that? D'ya say your
        name's Harvey?' Oh for fuck's sake, it's ARVIND! Rhymes
        with wind! I just can't face coming up with the same
        explanation I've had to repeat all my life. 'Not Harvey;
        ArvIND, it's an Indian name, my Dad comes from…yadda
        yadda yadda'… So instead I lean in towards her and say,
        'My name is… Abulkasem.'

C: Abulkasem?

B: Abukasem…

C: Abulkasem… You kidding? Is that really your name?

B: Yup!

C: Do you know there's an Abulkasem in the Arabian Nights?

B: (*Suddenly quite calm.*) 'Course. Doesn't everyone? Only
        it's best known from that play…You know Seniora Luna…
        by that Almqvist guy…' And then it just hits me like this
        fucking thunderbolt!… this total transformation takes
        place… Suddenly it's not girl-shy Arvind standing there…
        Not the Arvind who got bullied for stammering or his pouffy
        name… It's Abulkasem! I am Abulkasem… Like the name
        has taken over, filling me with calm… Abulkasem is like
        nang self-confident… Abulkasem doesn't get the sweats or
        the shakes, his knees don't wobble… Abulkasem just keeps
        the girl standing at the counter and starts pouring honey in
        her ears with these amazing compliments… 'You're…you're
        so lovely…So very lovely, you are… Really…'

C: (*Suddenly tender.*) Thanks… That was so sweet…

B: So Abulkasem starts telling her about his flashy
       telemarketing job… Abulkasem starts asking her interesting
       questions like he's some nang kind of pimp, so professional,
       you wouldn't believe… He offers her a cig and tells her cool
       jokes and tries to pay for her beer. There's this fantastic
       mood; the atmosphere is really cooking. Until she suddenly
       gets this guilt trip on account of her mates…

C: Listen, I've got to join my friends now… Only… Maybe we
       could chat a bit more later on?

B: And Abulkasem understands exactly what she means… You
       know by… 'Chat a bit more later on'… That's girl-talk…
       I swear she's on fire, she's got to have me. So I'm like,
       'Sure…why don't you give me your number and we can…
       chat later.'

C: Okay… I'll write it on this… Have a good time…only
       promise you'll ring…

       C leaves the stage, smiling flirtatiously.

B: On my life, that's the last thing she says before she walks
       over to her mates. And I just… Or Abulkasem just…or we
       both just stand there with her mobile number in our hands
       and then we slide back to Chas with a couple of freshly
       purchased Buds and drink a toast in bottled beer and
       everything is so incredibly beautiful you know the kind of
       night when everything just shines, everything is bright and
       alive and sparkling and you even feel like smiling at the
       blokes on the door… The kind of evening when the driver
       of the night bus lets you travel home for free and spring is
       in the air even though it's still winter and on the way home
       your mind keeps whispering… At last… Things are going
       to change at last… That was the kind of night it was… A
       wicked evening…

2 SCENE 2: THE EXPERTS (1)

The panel of experts on the subject of Abulkasem's birth.

A (GUIDE): (*Clears his throat.*) A very warm welcome to you all… Let me say how incredibly pleased I am to see so many of you here. You might like to think of me as… well… as your guide for the evening. A safe pair of hands to help you find your way through the performance and if there is anything that is unclear, absolutely anything at all, please don't hesitate to ask. Okay? Right then… And don't forget… there's no such thing as a stupid question…

Abulkasem…this figure shrouded in myth and legend…Who was he REALLY? What was his life like before he became one of the world's most wanted men? Why don't we start at the beginning and let's keep strictly to the facts. We're going to try and drill our way through the wall of fiction to get at the TRUTH about Abulkasem.

And helping us this evening is our panel of eminent experts. A round of applause for them, please.

(*B, C and D come onstage.*)

A: And a very warm welcome to you too… My first question… Where was Abulkasem born?

B (EXPERT 1): We think he was born in Tair Haifa, a village that lies in what is now southern Lebanon. Abulkasem's childhood has been portrayed in the television documentary 'Down from Day One' by Robin Alty.

C (EXPERT 2): (*Clears her throat.*) Though, then again, we have to bear in mind the findings of Hugo Sbeger, as presented in his excellent biography, 'The Radiance of Abulkasem', which point to Abulkasem actually having been born on Palestinian soil, in the village of al-Birwa.

D (EXPERT 3): If – that is – he wasn't born in Lubya or Iqrit, as Professor Chi Yen Deck maintains.

A: What do we know about his childhood? Was he shy? Aggressive? Did he have a lot of friends?

C: There's a remark by Hugo Sbeger that neatly captures the essence of Abulkasem's childhood which was, and I quote, 'as ordinary as a childhood can be without becoming exceptional by dint of its mediocrity' end quote.

D: Dr Cecil Zeenooza tells us that Abulkasem was the youngest of eight brothers and sisters. He was born, grew up and lived an entirely normal life in an entirely normal refugee camp.

A: So what was he like in school? Do we know anything about that?

B: In a dissertation presented at Wits University in Johannesburg, Alfred Dunmolds, one of the world's most celebrated experts in this field, wrote that Abulkasem would often sit in the middle of the classroom. Not right at the back and not right at the front.

C: He was the kind of person his classmates had difficulty remembering only a year or two after they'd left school.

D: A touch anonymous.

C: Somewhat shadowy.

B: Without any really distinguishing features.

C: The kind of person who soon gets reduced to leaving only a vague feeling of recognition, you know, like the classmate you meet in a lift ten years later and don't say hello to.

D: And it's only once you've got out of the lift that you realise why that person's face seemed so familiar.

B: Only by then the lift doors have closed and it's too late.

A: Ahem... So there is nothing about Abulkasem's childhood that would explain his violent future? No weapons? No fundamentalism?

C: Not to this point. As a young man, Abulkasem still remained naïve and unspoilt.

B: Although Chi Yen Deck does point out that Abulkasem's father was a very angry man. He used to beat his wife and he abused his daughters.

D: That's right: 'the perfect breeding-ground for terrorism' as Deck wrote in the biography published by Doubleday, the American publishing house, in 1987.

A: Terrorism, right. What do we actually know about Abulkasem's political involvement?

B: Robin Alty tells us that Abuklasem was 25 years old when he got a job as a columnist on the Arab newspaper El-Kharion. And it was then his problems began. Under a number of rather transparent bylines such as Akulbasem or Alubkasem, he started writing those controversial articles of his...

D: He praised the foreign policy of the US.

C: He defended the expansion of the Israeli settlements; he thanked the Israelis, a landless people, for taking pity on Palestine, that people-less land.

B: Even so, we know that – at the same time – Abulkasem was taking part in anti-American demonstrations, chanting anti-Semitic slogans and burning the Israeli flag. All this according to Hugo Sbeger.

A: That means... His articles were ironic... Doesn't it?

D: We think so...

B: But what we KNOW on the other hand is that from now on no one could trust Abulkasem.

C: He developed into a master of swings and roundabouts.

D: He soon became known among his countrymen as a collaborator...

C: And as a man of the resistance in the enemy camp.

B: The West came to see him as a potential terrorist.

C: The Arab world as a traitor.

D: Everyone read him as though he was their opponent.

B: And soon everyone was agreed that it was Abulkasem who posed the greatest threat to our common future.

A: And this was the point that efforts began to track him down?

C: Exactly.

A: Thank you so much… We'll take a break here… We'll be back after this…

3 SCENE 3: 'THE LEGENDARY DIRECTOR'

C remains on stage.

C: The monologue begins with me standing outside my door and swearing so loudly it can be heard right up the stairwell. Christ on a crutch, what a cunting cock. I've managed to lock myself out for the third time in two weeks. Bleeding buggering blockhead. Why does life have to be so…predictable?

I've been so good all week, worked hard for my exams, helped my brother move, kept away from the nightlife, I've been helping other people instead. As well as doing my exams… I've even defrosted the freezer. Mostly to avoid having to study it's true, but I mean. Can you actually imagine anyone being that good? And here I am all the same, bent over and covered in sweat, in riding boots that still squeak, looking through my own letter-box. Again. What a stupid sucking spastic mongrel!

So I pull myself together. I take some deep breaths. I decide to drop in at the bar my tutorial group are supposed to be at to celebrate finishing their exams. I actually intended to stay home only now I feel a hell of a lot more like a beer than calling out the locksmith. Again. He'd do that joke of his about my needing to buy shares in his company. Again. And I'd pretend-laugh in the hope of getting a discount. Again.

The bar we're supposed to meet at is called Kelly's, I don't know if you know it? A really crappy joint where they sell cheap beer. We're talking neon signs in the windows, pissed-off bouncers and cloakroom attendants who make you pay extra to leave your sweater tucked into the sleeve of your jacket. We're talking bottled beer in barrels, two quid a piece, Bon Jovi music, Chelsea fans and 40-year-olds in leather skirts. So in I roll. Looking round to find the other members of my tutorial group... I move towards the bar to order a... When all of a sudden I can feel someone pulling the shark-trick... You know what I mean... Someone sort of circling round, circling round you, with this hungry look...

B circles round C with the sexy look of a guy on the prowl.

Wouldn't you know it. Just what I need. A Turk in a leather jacket on the pull...

B samples his breath against the palm of his hand and moves in.

B (ARVIND): (*With a stammer.*) What's up, baby?

C: What?

B: What's up? My name's Abulkasem... So how's it going? What's going down?

C: What?

B: (*Stammering.*) Like I said... Abulkasem's the name...So how's it hanging, like?

C: Oh I see, okay I guess.

B: Chilled-like...

C: (*To the bartender.*) Hi there, could I get a Staropramen, please.

Embarrassing silence.

B: So...a'wight?

C: Fine thanks.

B: I like your boots.

C: Uh...thank you.

B: (*With a nod to the helmet.*) So you got a moped, then?

C: No.

B: Good.

C: Why's that good?

B: What?

C: Why's it good I haven't got a moped?

B: Well uh… I haven't got one either.

C: Really?

B: So we've got something in common. Though I have got my driving license, you know, and I can borrow the company car if I want.

C: Okay.

Embarrassing silence. C is given her beer.

B: I work in telemarketing… A cool job, like… Only not on commission… You've got to be a real sucker to work on commission… We get a guaranteed minimum wage, you see…

C: Sounds like fun…

B: In general like? You doing all right? Everything chilled-like?

C: Yes, it's all fine… And it still is…

Embarrassing silence. C looks round to try and find the members of her tutorial group.

B: Listen… So do you want something to drink like? My shout? Whatever you like?

C: Uh… No, I just ordered… Thank you.

B: So…you having fun tonight?

C: Ish.

B: So chilled like…

(*Silence.*)

C: Anyway listen, I'm going to…

B: Only you are really fine… I dig your style. Seriously, I mean it. You are really that fine… So can I get your number like?

C: What?

B: Can I get your number?

C: What do you want that for?

B: It's just, you know…we could hang a bit, chill, get together a bit more 'private' like. Are you up for that?

C: (*To the audience.*) Just to get rid of him, I scribble down some numbers on a napkin…

B: (*Thrilled.*) Cool… (*Looks at the piece of paper.*)… Hang about… Isn't there a number missing?

C: Oh, sorry… Here you are… There's a two on the end as well…

B: Cool… Anyway…I'll call you… And don't worry… I get free calls from work… I can make as many calls as I like… And that's only one of the perks of working in telemarketing…

C: And that's when I catch sight of my tutorial group at last. The Turk backs off to his mates smiling his big smile and shooting off imaginary pistols…

        Smiling, B backs offstage – his hands shaped to form pistols which he shoots off in the air.

        There they are. My very own tutorial group.

        The journalist on the local rag who says he's taking a 'time-out' to do a course in theatre studies.

        (*A (**THE JOURNALIST**) waves to C.*)

        The old girl wearing the necklace of African beads with an unrequited love of education who simply adores Simon Callow.

        (*D (**THE AFRICAN BEADS LADY**) waves at C.*)

        And then there's the Scot who is determined to read all the set texts from a post-colonial perspective and never stops, one seminar after the other, dropping the name of Franz Fanon.

        (*B (**THE FANON FAN**) nods towards C.*)

        I pull up a chair at the narrow end of the table, have a sip of beer and listen to the conversations. The discussions

are really very spirited, incredibly interesting. We drink our
beers and ask one another how we are…

A, D AND B: (*All at the same time.*) Fine thanks, can't complain,
mustn't grumble, getting by, the same old aches and pains,
just toddling along, you know how it is. Thank God it's
Friday, and how's tricks?

Short pause.

C: All the same…

A, D AND B: (*All at the same time.*) Well, I mean, you're bound to
be a bit tired, we're all a bit tired, well exhausted actually,
you could almost say we're burnt-out, couldn't you.

C: We drink some more beer and agree that yesterday's test
was very hard.

A, D AND B: (*All at the same time.*) It was really hard, very tricky,
unbelievably difficult.

C: Though it was pretty easy at the same time, wasn't it?

A, D AND B: (*All at the same time.*)Wasn't it just, I suppose you'd
have to say it was pretty easy really.

B: (*Scots accent.*) And POWERFULLY influenced by a colonial
and Eurocentric perspective…

C: …says the Fanon Fan. And we keep on like that for an hour
or two. More beer and blah blah blah with nothing at all
being said. Until the journalist turns to me and wants to talk
about origins.

A: Listen…there's this thing I've been wondering about…
Where do you actually come from? So, your parents are
Kurds? Kurdistania, eh? I live out in the suburbs myself.
We've got a really fascinating mix of people there. Just by
way of example, one of my neighbours…he's from Pakistan.
But really pleasant. Just incredibly nice, in fact.

C: There goes the starting pistol. For a subject I've had to
endure a thousand times and that I never seem able to
escape. As Dad used to say, 'When the locals want to talk

about origins, they start spouting like volcanoes – there's no putting them out.'

D: (*Sighs – touches C's hair.*) Oh – Kurdistan. You must have had such a difficult time… Growing up split like that between two so INCREDIBLY different cultures. You poor little thing.

A: So I said to my neighbour: Fine by me, you can eat your own kind of food and have that satellite dish on the balcony. Only please, please, don't force your daughter to wear a veil when she grows up. Please don't. Do it for me. Let her be free. That's what I said. I didn't mince my words.

D: (*To C.*) Just like a suspension bridge dangling between the two sides of a cultural abyss.

B: (*Scots.*) Female circumcision… Now that's where I have to draw the line. There's just no way I'm prepared to support that.

D: (*Touching C's hair.*) And the only thing you can do is hang there, dangling in mid-air, like some poor iced-up suspension bridge, shivering in the freezing cold. Neither one thing nor the other. It's just too sad.

C: And ten minutes later they're totally absorbed in a debate about honour killings. One of them refers to the oppression of women and another mentions satellite dishes and someone else suicide bombers. I try and stonewall them into silence. But it doesn't seem to be working this time.

D: So what do you think about the Muslim cultural tradition?

A: What kind of relationship do you have with your father? What would he say if he could see you here, with us? With that (*Nods towards the beer bottle.*)?

C: 'Cheers, maybe,' I say and try to change the subject. But I get nowhere.

B: (*Scots accent.*) Do you feel that you're under threat from your family since you've chosen to live the Western way?

D: Let me give you a hug. You need to have a good cry – safe and warm within my arms.

A: I can completely understand that it must be unbelievably difficult for a woman to make her own way in an environment that is so defined by the traditional.

C: (*To the audience.*) That was the moment I'd had enough. But I just refuse to submit this time. I start telling them about the opposition, about secular cultural circles within Muslim society, about the intellectuals, about veiled postmodernist radical feminists. And then I play my trump card.

'And of course you'll all have heard of...of...' I'm just about to tell them about my new idol, aren't I, about the Muslim theatre director Aouatef who had a worldwide success with her stagings of *Endgame* and *The Hamlet Machine*. She was the one who inspired me to do theatre studies. She's one of the up-and-coming superstars of the theatrical world. Only...all of a sudden I get this blackout. Her name has gone blank. And I hear myself saying instead,

'And of course you'll all heard of...of...of...A...A – A – Abulkasem, haven't you?'

What was I supposed to do? I had to say something. And it was only later on I realised that I had borrowed the name from that Turk in the leather jacket.

D AND B: Abulkasem?

C: Oh come on, you must have heard about the theatre director Abulkasem? You are doing theatre studies, aren't you?

A: Ah! Now I get it. AbulKASem, so that's how you pronounce it. It's all coming together now. Yeah, I've heard of him.

C: It's a her.

A: That's right. I just said that. I've heard a lot about her.

C: And then I tell them everything I know about Aouatef. Only I call her Abulkasem. I tell them about her celebrated staging of *Ubu Roi*, which toured the whole of the Middle East for five years. I tell them about the recent article in the New York Times which referred to her as 'a real gift to the future

35

of theatre'. I tell them she's a close friend of Oliver Sacks and Jonathan Miller.

A: Wow. Miller...

C: I've got them in the palm of my hand. There aren't any neon lights, no sad idiots on the prowl, no Bon Jovi from the loudspeakers. There's just me telling tales from Abulkasem's life. Abulkasem, the legendary director from the Arab world who always turns up at her premieres in various disguises. The woman with a particular predilection for violet pashminas and silver-coloured monocles. Their ears prick up when I tell them about Abulkasem being lauded by Peter Brook when she was awarded the British International Theatre Award in 2002.

A: Oh yes, that's right. I remember that too. There was a lot of media attention.

C: I end by telling them what happened the time Aouatef... or Abulkasem, I mean, was in New York for the first time setting up *Six Characters in Search of an Author*. 'Didn't you hear about that? It was early on in her career. One night she was at a jazz club and caught sight of Woody Allen. She wanted to go over to him and say hello, but felt too shy. She didn't feel brave enough, more like some sad groupie. She went over to the bar instead and ordered a drink to calm herself down. And then she went over to Woody's table, her legs shaking.' They all listen in silence. 'She reached out her hand and introduced herself, "Excuse me Mr Allen... Sorry to disturb you, but my name is Abulkasem and I would just like to thank you for your movies and..." And Woody Allen just laughed and shouted to everyone around him, "Hey, guys, I TOLD you it was Abulkasem!"

I look them in the eyes and they laugh and I smile and the whole thing just couldn't be any better. The only one not laughing is that journalist guy...

A: But...wasn't it Ingmar Bergman that happened to...? He was the one who met Woody Allen in New York and... Come on, pull the other one.

Brief pause.

C: There's this very peculiar silence around the table. One of
        them clears their throat. Someone coughs. Someone else
        scratches their neck. And so what do I do? 'Exactly. That's
        what's so crazy about the whole thing. That it happened to
        both Bergman and to Aouatef!'

D: Who's Aouatef?

C: Abulkasem.

B: Who's Ingmar Bergman?

C: What the fuck difference does it make?

B: Right. Sorry.

C: There's silence for a minute or two. Then I get up on
        wobbly legs and say goodbye. It isn't until I get home that I
        remember that I'm still locked out.

        Fucking faggot cunting cock of an arse-licking mother-
        fucker. I sink into a squat outside the door… You moronic
        jism of a jackass, you shit-eating sewer rat… I ring
        the locksmith… Confound it to hell, you contemptible
        incompetent. My stock of swearwords starts to run dry.
        Bombs and grenades, drop the damn shades. I peer in
        through the letter-box and whisper… Slutty slattern…
        Nefarious nincompoop… Imbecillic idiot… I fall asleep…I
        dream about Aouatef… She is standing on a stage with a
        gigantic bouquet in her arms. The audience are applauding
        like mad, flashlights going off. Aouatef waves and smiles.
        A shimmering violet shawl around her neck and a steely
        gleam of silver from one of her eyes. A monocle.

4 SCENE 4: THE EXPERTS (2)

*The panel of experts on the subject of Abulkasem's
escape.*

A (GUIDE): A warm welcome back… We're going to take another
        look at the real Abulkasem… His columns have made him
        a hate figure on all sides… The PLO have labelled him

a collaborator. Mossad – a terrorist. The CIA – an illegal combatant. So what's next?

B (EXPERT 1): This is where we come into the picture. We've been entrusted with the task of keeping watch, and an extra attentive watch at that, on Abulkasem.

C (EXPERT 2): Which is exactly what we are doing.

D (EXPERT 3): We're dogging his every step.

A: The world against Abulkasem. Round one...

B: We watch him as he packs his suitcases, getting ready to go on the run.

D: Not that we ever let him out of our sight.

C: He soon notices he is being tailed.

B: He starts tearing peep-holes in newspapers to be able to keep an eye on the entrance to the café where he drinks his morning coffee.

C: He starts putting on disguises...

B: Monocles and eye-patches, veils and false mustaches.

D: He does everything he can to confuse us...

C: But that doesn't stop us keeping track of him. We can see through his disguises and we're just waiting for our orders...

B: Abulkasem hasn't slept for several weeks.

D: Only the same day our orders arrive, Abulkasem manages to buy a bus ticket to Istanbul...

C: And just to confuse us, he gives the ticket to his brother.

The pace quickens.

D: The same moment the bus is blown up by a dumbed-down smart bomb, Abulkasem crosses the border into Jordan.

B: From Jordan he hitchhikes to Senegal; in Dakar he steals onboard a vessel that is transporting freon freezers and Happy-Meal figures to South America.

Music.

D: And we're right on his heels.

C: Abulkasem is soon working as a monkey smuggler in Porto
        Alegre. Following a police raid, he goes on the run again.
        He moves northwards joined by Hamama the monkey.
        He puts together a raft out of driftwood, floats down the
        Amazon to Belém, where he sells Hamama to a film
        producer on the lookout for a monkey – in exchange for a
        flight to Houston.

B: It is a curious fact that this is the same monkey who plays
        Marcel, Ross' monkey, in the television series Friends.

STAGE HAND: Will you be going on much longer?

A: Sorry.

        A goes off in search of the technician.

D: We're right on his heels.

B: Our agents have been despatched.

C: Individuals who look like policemen pretending to read
        week-old newspapers. Perfumed women with cameras in
        their make-up mirrors. Dwarf agents disguised as children.

D: Though Abulkasem still manages to give them the slip…
        He disguises his voice; he mixes together every conceivable
        language, Urdu with Zembli with Persian with West
        Country…

B: He pretends to stammer; he pretends to be mute; he
        pretends to be a Spaniard in Chinatown and a Frenchman
        in Little Italy.

C: He alters his smell… One day he smells strongly of
        sweat, on another he reeks of Fahrenheit and Kenzo and
        Obsession.

D: He keeps changing the location of his crescent-shaped
        birthmark. On some days it is on his left cheek, on others
        on the right one. Sometimes you can see it on his forehead,
        sometimes it has slid down on to one of his elbows.

C: And one time when he wakes up in a hotel room in Arizona
        whose walls are stained by damp, he actually puts make-up

over the original birthmark and then places a false one on EXACTLY the same spot.

A: Yes, but what about you lot? Are you still after him?

B: The whole time… We keep hunting him down with laser sights and radar, satellite imaging and smart bombs.

C: We're manufacturing a special version of the Memory game in which all the images represent Abulkasem in various disguises…

D: Abulkasem as an apple-picker.

B: Abulkasem as Lance, the professional dancer.

D: Abulkasem as Arvind, the telemarketing salesman with a stammer.

B: Abulkasem as Aouatef, the legendary woman director.

C: On the other side of the cards, you are reminded of the six-figure reward being offered and the telephone number for providing the police with information…

A: Listen the thing is, I'm not sure I…or the audience understand… Why it is Abulkasem in particular that is so important? What has he actually done? What does Sbeger have to say about that? Zeenooza? Dunmolds? After all, there must be some kind of…evidence?

D,C and B squirm in their seats.

So why him in particular?

D, C and B reading out loud at the same time and at a very fast pace:

D: As a washer-up he works his way round Asia until he gets to Europe. He steals off the boat in the French town of Boulogne, hires a tramp-steamer that takes him up to The Hague, borrows a banana boat which takes him on to the Dutch city of Harleem, rents jetskis which whisk him along the Rhine, hops on a ski-lift over the Alps, travels down the other side in a black rubbish bag. A tractor helps him to cross the marshes of Lake Constance, and another lorry driver takes him on to Innsbruck.

B: He leaves Spain behind on a coach, an Audi 100 takes him to Toulouse, a parachute catapult thrusts him up onto the Central Massif, a boxcar drives him down to Saint-Etienne. He makes his way to Stuttgart by bike, and then to Heidelberg on a delivery moped, he completes the whole onward route to Bremen on roller-skates.

C: He gets a lift on a juggernaut to Basel, a friendly hang-glider gets him past Lichtenstein. He jogs up to the Danish border, he moonlight-flits through Jutland, cartwheels along to Odense and crawls backwards toward Copenhagen and swims the butterfly over the Sound to Malmö.

Brief pause.

D: And for the last stretch – from Malmö to Stockholm – he takes a high-speed train, the X2000, peak period!

C: So now he's here…

B: In our midst…

D: And chaos awaits us…

A: It's just… What I…what we don't quite understand…is… why Abulkasem in particular? Maybe we'll get an answer to that soon… After this perhaps…

SCENE 5: 'THE APPLE-PICKER'

A is alone onstage.

VOICE OF AN ANSWERING MACHINE: You have one new message…

B'S (ARVIND'S) VOICE: What's up, baby. This is Abulkasem again… the guy you met at Kelly's… Anyway… I'm not sure if you got my other messages only… I just thought I'd ring again to check if you…that you'd got them, like. It'd be kind of fun…cool, I mean, if you could ring me so we could hang together, like, chill a bit… You know… You're really nice… I'm really nice… We could be really nice together, couldn't we? Ring me so we can meet up… Hope you're having a good time… Chilled, like.

VOICE OF AN ANSWERING MACHINE: Message received the…

A (APPLE-PICKER): (*Very pronounced accent.*) Many dreamings, me sick... NOT feel good... NOT good head... WAR in head, yes? WAR. Many thinkings not good... Many dreamings NOT good, many not-sleepings... Understand? Not? Mine head not good... Not happy, not calm, not many sleepings, many wakings, many waitings. Sweaty. Many sweaty, you understand? Night not sleeping just waiting. Days picking apple, picking apples. Understand? Wait lawyer phone. Lawyer gone. No one phone. No one phone, always silent. Just picking apples. Suddenly someone phone. Again and Again. Not lawyer. Other not know... Someone phone again and again, listen this... Listen:

VOICE OF AN ANSWERING MACHINE: You have three new messages:

B'S VOICE: Hi there. This is Abulkasem. Again. Is this really your number or not? Lara? Call me back now. What's going on? Why did you give me your number if you're not going to call me back? What? Hello? Give me a call, please...

VOICE OF AN ANSWERING MACHINE: Message received the...

A: Is who? Not know. Who Abulkasem? He persecuting... He phone again and again and again... He phoning every day now... Saying 'I am Abulkasem'. 'This is Abulkasem.' Is who? Dreamings not good, Abulkasem not good... War in head. In day picking apples. In night I dreaming Abulkasem... Abulkasem hunting... I dreaming no one understand my words... I dreaming I ask: You have interpreter? You have interpreter? Get interpreter! I dreaming interpreter come.

C comes on stage. ALL of A's lines are said in PERSIAN (apart from the song-texts in English, of course) and interpreted into English by C.

A: (*In Persian.*) *I'd like to start by saying what a great honour it is for me to be able to tell you my story.*

C (INTERPRETER): I'd like to start by saying what a great honour it is for me to be able to tell you my story.

A: (*In Persian.*) *To reduce the risk of any linguistic misunderstanding I have chosen to tell my story in Persian.*

C: To reduce the risk of any linguistic misunderstanding I have chosen to tell my story in Persian.

A: *And for those of you who do not speak Persian we have an interpreter with us, who will be translating my story.*

C: And for those of you who do not speak Persian we have an interpreter with us (*Points to herself.*) who will be translating my story.

A: *I arrived in Sweden four years ago.*

C: I arrived in Sweden four years ago.

A: *I fell in love with this wonderful country…*

C: I fell in love with this wonderful country…

A: *I wanted to stay here for ever…*

C: I wanted to stay here forever…

A: *But my application hearing for asylum kept on being delayed…*

C: But my application hearing for asylum kept on being delayed…

A: *I made an effort to settle into the detention centre… I stayed calm… But after my first appeal was rejected everything changed…*

C: I made an effort to settle into the detention centre… I stayed calm… But after my first appeal was rejected everything changed…

A: *I had difficulty sleeping… I felt persecuted… I ran away from the centre and hid in a house in the south… I picked apples and waited for my lawyer to call me…*

C: I had difficulty sleeping…I felt persecuted…I ran away from the centre and hid in a house in the south…I picked apples and waited for my lawyer to call me…

A: *No call ever came… Time passed… One season after another… I remained in hiding… I made myself invisible… I stopped existing…*

C: No call ever came... Time passed... One season after another... I remained in hiding... I made myself invisible... I stopped existing...

A: *Silence all around me... I can hear my own thoughts... I am waiting... They will be coming soon... I can feel it...*

C: Silence all around me... I can hear my own thoughts... I am waiting... They will be coming soon... I can feel it...

A: *Then one day my mobile rings! At last! Only it is not the lawyer... Instead it is someone who calls himself Abulkasem... Abulkasem? I'd never heard that name before... Who is he? I stop answering but the mobile just goes on ringing... Day after day for almost a fortnight...*

C: Then one day my mobile rings! At last! Only it is not the lawyer... Instead it is someone who calls himself Abulkasem... Abulkasem? I'd never heard that name before... Who is he? I stop answering but the mobile just goes on ringing... Day after day for almost a fortnight...

A: *I can't sleep... I am waiting... I can't answer when it rings... I start to realise... It's all the fault of fucking Sweden... I start hating Sweden...*

C: (*Noticeably irritated.*) I can't sleep... I am waiting... I can't answer when it rings...I start to realise... It's all the fault of fucking Sweden... I start hating Sweden...

Brief pause; A starts to smile; C now starts making alterations to A's story.

A: *The only thing that can still console me is the music...*

C: But Sweden is nevertheless a great deal better than my homeland.

A: *The music has always been there and it has never abandoned me...*

C: There was quite a lot of terrorist activity in my background.

A: *Saber, my youngest brother and I, had a rock group when we were little...*

C: Saber, my youngest brother and I, used to pretend to be
       suicide bombers even when we were very young...

A: *Now when everything has become so difficult to deal with,
       I can always count on music to come to my rescue...I
       get out the old music cassette my uncle sent me from
       Canada...*

C: My father was very cruel, I decided to turn my hatred of my
       father against the world around me. And that's how I got
       involved in politics.

       *A is so caught up in his story that he fails to pay attention
       to C's translation.*

A: *The cassette was actually meant as a present for my
       mother... But she passed it on to me and it soon became
       mine... just for me...*

C: I have a very firm Muslim faith and my hatred of the US is
       (*Tries to find the words.*) ...spontaneously combustible...or
       in any case...very, very powerful...

A: *The tape contained an assortment of hits and gave me the
       key to a new world: the world of music.*

C: However the hatred I feel towards Americans bears no
       comparison with the infernal depths of my hatred of Jews...

A: *It was owing to this cassette that I was tempted into leaving
       my homeland and I moved to Europe to try and become an
       opera singer.*

C: There is no people I loathe more than the Jews... To
       begin with this was largely for political reasons but then it
       became...how to put it...more personal. I really do loathe
       them. Their curls... Their long noses... That loathsome
       meanness of theirs...

A: *So what was on that cassette? Pavarotti? Domingo? Jussi
       Björling?*

C: Just like the real Abulkasem, I took part in anti-American
       demonstrations, chanted anti-Semitic slogans and burnt the
       Israeli flag.

A: *Aida? Porgy and Bess? Der Rosenkavalier? Oh no, not
       at all! I'll give you four clues: Björn, Benny, Agneta and
       Frida… It was ABBA!*

C: There was this one time I was being interviewed on Spanish
       television about the Oslo peace process. And I yelled at
       them that neither Abulkasem nor I would ever surrender
       until the last Jew had been thrown out of Palestine.

A: *(With a nostalgic smile.) Mm… ABBA, the first Greatest
       Hits album. I couldn't get enough of it; I played that
       cassette night and day. All the great hits were on it…Super
       Trouper, Knowing Me Knowing You, The Winner Takes It
       All…*

C: As already mentioned, we took part in demonstrations, we
       chanted slogans, burnt the American and Israeli flags.

A: *I remember the way I used to walk round the streets of
       my home city singing (He sings.) 'Mamma mia, here I go
       again, my my how can I resist you… Mamma mia, does it
       show again, my my, just how much I've missed you…'*

C: And, just like Abulkasem, it wasn't long before I began to
       dream about blowing myself up.

A: *Or that one (Sings.) 'Like a bang-a-boom-bommerang,
       dummi-dum-dummi, dummi-dum-dum, a bang-a-boome-
       boomerang, love is a tune you hummy-hum-hum…'*

C: I contacted the Al-Aqsa Brigade and volunteered to be a
       martyr.

       *A loses his thread, looks at C, realises that she is not telling
       his story, tests her:*

A: *Other songs on the cassette… Chiquita… Fernando… The
       Name of the Game…*

C: My goal – to murder as many defenceless Jews as possible.
       The thing I wanted most was a bloodbath!

       *A not singing but reeling off lines of text as though they
       were questions.*

A: *Waterloo – 'I was defeated, you won the war? Waterloo promise to love you forever more?'*

C: Before I tied the dynamite belt around my waist, I recorded a valedictory message on video in which I praised the prophet Mohammed.

A: *'So when you're near me?*
Darling can't you hear me?'

C: I also said that all Western women are whores.

A: (*Mumbling.*) SOS?

A falls silent and looks at C.

C: I broadcast a greeting to another great man of action: Hitler.

Pause as though she were waiting for A to finish talking.

I rounded things off by saying that the attack on the World Trade Centre was one vast plot on the part of Jewish conspirators, the whole thing orchestrated to make the US go to war against the Arab world.

Pause as though she were waiting for A to finish talking.

When the videotape was finished, I fastened the dynamite belt around my body and left my home.

Pause as though she were waiting for A to finish talking.

I was thinking things like: female circumcision – a lovely tradition that should be spread across the entire world.

Pause as though she were waiting for A to finish talking.

I was struck by the idea that the clitoris is really like a rosebush… It has to be pruned if it is to blossom.

Pause as though she were waiting for A to finish talking.

And I thought, if I had son, he would be called Saddam. Or Osama. Or both. Sort of like a double-barrelled name.

C exits.

Silence.

A: (*In English to the audience.*) Not more war... Not good...
Many war, many violence... Interpreter not good... War
not good... Abulkasem not good... I waiting four years...
I finish waiting... Maybe asylum, maybe torture... Maybe
prison... No one know... Not good... head feel bad...
Lawyer gone... Lawyer idiot. Now me head sick...
Abulkasem everywhere... Watching... Threatening... Maybe
I Abulkasem? Maybe you Abulkasem?

Silence...looks at the audience with suspicion.

Who Abulkasem? You? Maybe you Abulkasem? Head much
tired. Little sleepings. Many many wakings.

VOICE OF THE ANSWERING MACHINE: You have one new
message...

SCENE 6: THE EXPERTS (3)

*The panel of experts on the subject of Abulkasem's time
in Sweden.*

A (GUIDE): (*Ingratiating.*) So how are you all out there? Everything
okay? Not long left now... Everyone still with us? Are you
sitting comfortably? Does anyone have any questions?
Good! So let's get on. My final question: What happens
when Abulkasem arrives in Sweden? And let's not bother
with... Chi Yen Deck and Sbeger and Zeenooza...and
whatever their names are. What we are interested in
are YOUR findings. What do YOU have to say about
Abulkasem's time in Sweden?

B (EXPERT 1): Let's take a look at Slide numero uno.

*They all look backstage as though an image had
appeared.*

And there you have it!

He turns towards the audience.

This is the first pictorial proof we have of Abulkasem
actually entering Sweden. It was taken by a Chinese family
on holiday, as you can see for yourselves. Why there they

are, a smiling Mum Dad and kid, three unsuspecting rice-eaters, posing for a picture in the compartment of an X2000 high-speed train... Only just whose silhouette is that, do you think? Lurking in the background? You've got it... Abulkasem on his way to Stockholm... He was trying to steal in without being seen but oh no you don't, no sirree... And now let's take a look at the consequences for us of his coming to our shores.

D (EXPERT 3): Abulkasem has crossed the border and immediately there is a rise in the number of rapes...

C: There is a marked increase in the sale of garlic.

D: Thefts of batteries soar.

C: Sesame seeds...

D: Insurance frauds...

C: And the number of pot-holes in our city streets just continues to climb.

B: Uhm, right...which brings us to our last image...

   (*The sound of slides changing.*)

   Here you can see Abulkasem in July 2000 when he was finally arrested by the Swedish police in the south of the country. He was working for £1.50 an hour as part of an apple-picking operation when we grabbed him...ripe for the plucking, as you might say... This photo, which I'm sure is familiar to you all, was taken on the day of the trial, just before Abulkasem got deported, sent back to wherever it was he came from... Here you can see all the detainees being led into to the courtroom and Abulkasem is...now let me see... I admit it is a bit difficult to tell them apart but...that one is Abulkasem...that's got to be him...the fourth one from the left with the bandaged fingers... The one whose head is covered by a white cowboy hat...

   He inspects the wall at the back of the stage.

   Yup, that's our man...plucked like a rotten apple...

   He looks at the back wall.

…then again it could be that one…no, no that's him right enough… Well, there you have it…

A: Hrm… A big thank you to our panel of experts…and now… the last monologue of the evening.

SCENE 7: 'A KID BROTHER'S ENDING'

[Translator's note: it should be apparent to the audience that the language 'Kid Brother' is using is not his mother tongue]

D approaches the edge of the stage, he closes his eyes while B and C tell the story.

C: The time has come for X [*Actor's name.*] to take on the role of the playwright's youngest brother. He approaches the edge of the stage and keeps looking the audience straight in the eye.

B: He begins by telling us about something he remembers from last year. He has promised to come up with ideas for his elder brother's play but has had problems getting started. His imagination is blocked. He goes into the kitchen to make himself some sandwiches and some chocolate milk.

C: He comes back and sits on the sofa; he puts the telly on. His notebook is lying there beside him; the audience can see that he has written 'INVASION: Good title'.

B: Kid Brother zaps between channels. He ends up in the middle of a news item about attempted suicides among asylum seekers. The audience can hear the voice of the journalist talking about the Iranian who tried to set himself on fire in Gimo, the 17-year-old Somali who took 30 Valium tablets, the Russian who was found dead in the Uddevalla detention centre.

C: This is followed by a series of photos from controversial legal cases… And there he is! That's when he sees him. The photo of the asylum-seeking apple picker who was arrested in southern Sweden. The man who refused to give his real name. The man whose fingerprints could not be identified. The man who stubbornly insisted his name was… Abulkasem…

B: Kid brother gets up off the sofa, the notebook falls to the floor.

C: He can see a blurred black and white photo. But that is him, it has to be him, doesn't it?

B: The same moustache, the same droopy eyes, the same crescent-shaped birthmark.

C: And now a flood of memories overwhelms him.

B: And now he can smell burnt flesh.

C: And now he can hear something sizzling.

B: And now he writes down the person's name in his notebook. A-bul-ka-sem…

C: And now he reaches out for his mobile to text his big brother.

B: 'Got an idea for a play, ring me when home,' he writes; send message, message sent.

C: And now we'll hand you over to X [*Actor's name.*].

D opens his eyes; he speaks rhythmically, melodically, at a fast pace, as though in a trance; he catches his breath in the breaks.

D (KID BROTHER): I remember it wasn't that long ago, it was the summer holidays in Year Nine, you know, late hanging-arounds at McDonalds, it was pie and coffee for 99p, it was 'go on, hand us over that fifty p, bruv', it was 'ey, down and out, you already owe me,' it was 'Pay you back next week, I swear, on my mother's life'. It was scribbling swearwords on the place-mats, telling made-up stories about sex 'til it was closing time, knocking off paper napkins and straws to take out onto the streets.

Brief pause.

It was riding the night bus in circles, it was shooting wads at the necks of white boys what'd fallen asleep drunk, it was trying to pull chicks wearing Ugg boots, it was blagging cigs at bus-stops, it was going home when dawn came up over the city bridges and the city filled up with red. It was saying 'salaam aleikum' at the entrance to Ibrahim's building and it was 'talk to you tomorrow' and it was me and Peter walking home to the courtyard on our estate and then it was Peter saying 'salaam aleikum' and it came out perfect even though he comes from a family that's as Swedish as they come, a family that drives a Volvo and has a cottage in the country, with marinated herrings in the fridge and their true-blue daily Swedish newspaper delivered to their door with the first post every morning.

Brief pause.

It was summer holidays in Year Nine and Ibrahim went away on a charter plane and me and Peter was the only ones left in town. Peter's Mum, who was like the nicest Mum of all the mums, said to me,

Standard accent.

'We'd love to have you join us in the country, for a weekend or so; you'd be getting out of town a bit, getting some fresh country air. It'll do you good.'

It was the first time in my life I'd been invited to someone's place in the country 'cos there wasn't nobody in my class what had one. And before I went, I remember Dad packing a load of food as presents along with this extra large container of halva and he made me promise to be ever so polite and to be sure to say thank you more than once and take off my shoes and eat up every meal…even if they dished up pork.

Brief pause.

Then we was in their Volvo 740, Peter's baldy-Dad doing the driving and Peter's nicey-Mum singing along to Sting-tracks on the stereo and Peter's kid sister playing her gameboy and Peter just sitting there all pissed-off and quiet-like. Their cottage was down south and it was just like I'd imagined it, you know, all on its own with a separate garage and a little wood and a letter-box on the high road and pinecones all over the ground. And just like you'd expect they had loads of painted wellies for the little kids just like in a fairy-tale.

Brief pause.

And I remember the only thing that wasn't how I'd imagined it was Peter. When he was with us in the gang, he was always a bit of a saddo, you know the ginger bloke with freckles who gets picked on first if someone wants to start a fight, the little guy who gets eaten alive in one on one in basketball. The kid who only tries it on with the teacher if they're doing supply and always has to be the look-out if something's going to get nicked. Only now in the country he seemed different-like and several times I thought 'Shit, the way he is to his parents is just like we is to him!' When his Dad said he should help carry in the bags, Peter was like 'sure, laters' and left. Then when his Mum said he should lay the table, Peter just sighed and was like 'So what kind of fucking holiday is this, then?' And there was this one time at breakfast on the second day Peter called his own nicey-Mum a whore! I can understand you thinking I'm making this up, but walla it's true; at the breakfast table the next morning he called his very own nicey-Mum: fucking whore. Okay maybe he did say it a bit quiet like: 'fucking whore' but he really said it. I thought my ears were lying 'cos I could never have been believing what I was hearing.

Brief pause.

Then it was a bit later on and I remember Peter said we should do their summer tradition and take buckets down to the jetty and go fishing for crabs. Everything around us was like all sunshiney and jolly happy and butterflies and bees and flowers I didn't know the name of was making the path through the woods light up. On the way down to the lake we could see these big red-coloured buildings made out of rotting wood where cows and their kids used to live only now they were just for storing hays and dried-up old wasp-nests and I can remember Peter said we should hit the wasp nests with sticks 'cos that was a summer tradition as well and there was this crunching kind of sound and we got away without being bit. Then down by the water we started the crab-hunt and I can remember I ask Peter how you could say things like that to your Mum. 'If I did that to mine she'd strangle me to death then she'd bring me back to life just to strangle me all over again,' I said. Peter just came back silent and the crab-fishing was all we thought about for the rest of the day.

Brief pause.

Only when that day was more afternoon like, Peter said we should go and check out their neighbour's house what was a bit closer to the forest. This was a summer tradition too like and we picked up our buckets and I followed Peter's back while he told me the last few years their neighbours' house had filled up with these shady characters; there was this rumour the house was being used to hide secret refugees. Sometimes there was African families living there and the summer before there had been Kosovo Albanians and even though they was supposed to be secretly invisible they always had a fire going in the fireplace, even on sunny days, and Peter was like probably it was to burn corpses or smuggle out drugs or do voodoo to keep the spirits away. Sunlight was coming through the trees like a sieve and the birdsong sang and an owl hooted but I could kind of feel inside like there was this shivering cold. 'Ey, bruv, so what are doing going to disturb your neighbours. Isn't it time for dinner-time soon, Pete?' But Peter just kept on going. 'Chicken, are you?' (*Imitates the sound of a chicken.*) So we just kept on going, jumped over the ditch and crossed a tiny reddish river on a thin plank and then we was on someone's land with all this uncut grass and buildings that used to be dark blue but had got all spotted with brown.

Brief pause.

Peter crouched down like a soldier and crept over to the house and I done the same and tried to stop the crab bucket making any noise. We plucked up courage while we was crouching down under the kitchen window and

then cautious like we lifted up our heads and looked in.
The kitchen was like Peter's Mum's, only a bit bigger, there
wasn't nothing special to say that a ghost or any secrets
was hiding there. Over by the stove was this old guy, who
was maybe 50, and I can remember he had chinos on that
was beige and a white shirt with rolled-up sleeves and a
little brown waistcoat. There was a birthmark on one of
his cheeks, a bit like the shape of a moon. I was thinking
he was Turk but also he could be Iranian, maybe Arab. He
was standing by the stove with two white bowls and he
poured oil into one and he filled up the other with water
and the hotplate was on and I remember it was redder
than hotplates usually are and I remember the old guy was
rubbing his hands and I remember he seemed nervous
and I remember he was like waiting for someone and I
remember he took this huge deep breath and I remember
then he pressed the fingers of his hand right down on top of
the hotplate and I remember the sound of sizzling and his
eyes getting bigger and then all scrunched up and he kept
his hand on it and it sizzled some more and I remember
him using his other hand to steady himself and he still had
his fingers on the hotplate and there was smoke coming
off it and the old guy's arm jerked and his face was like a
wrung-out dishcloth and he closed his eyes and groaned
and his fingertips was burning and he kept them there
and I remember the tears on his cheeks and the smell of
fried sausage and I remember our breaths steaming up the
window-pane and Peter's face all flushed and red – like he
had make-up on – and I bit my lip until I could taste blood
and my heart was pounding and everything else was silent
except for some owl-sounds and the sizzling from the burnt
finger-flesh and when the old guy finally lifted his hand off
the hotplate and cooled his fingertips in the little bowl he
just happened to look up and his hand was shaking and his
eyes was all mixed up, water like and something red and…

Brief pause.

And I remember Peter screaming with fear and I did
the same and we rushed off into the woods, our steps

chattering like we were galloping crazy-like and we just kept going, we jumped over the stream, we flew over the ditch and my heart was going to explode and my tongue was like shredded by sandpaper and...

Brief pause.

And I remember we didn't stop until we were back on Peter's home turf and we didn't tell nobody nothing and Peter's Mum said it didn't matter we'd left the crab-buckets at the lake, we could fetch them tomorrow and then she said dinner would be ready soon and maybe you boys can help lay the table and both me and Peter helped and Peter's Mum was all pleased and surprised and like happy to the max and stroked our cheeks and said thank you and then she said she would make an extra-nice dessert with ice-cream, bananas, chocolate sauce and marshmallows, only first...first we're going to grill some sausages, she said... and smiled her nicest smile.

Pause. D shuts his eyes again.

C: Kid brother remains standing right at the front of the stage.

B: He looks out across the audience.

C: He leaves the stage.

    D remains standing where he is, still with his eyes shut.

A: Silence. Gradual darkness.

    Pause. The stage is abruptly plunged into darkness.

    END

Here's the Secret Answer to the Riddle of those Names:Changing the letters turns Hugo Sbeger into George Bush; Chi Yen Deck becomes Dick Cheney; Alfred Dumolds is Donald Rumsfeld,while Dr Cecil Zeenooza becomes Condoleezza Rice and Robin Alty is unmasked as Tony Blair.

THIS CHILD

By Joël Pommerat

Translated by Nigel Gearing

Further Copyright Information

Cet Enfant / This Child

Joël Pommerat is hereby identified as author of *Cet Enfant* in accordance with section 77 of the Copyright, Designs and Patents Act 1988. The author has asserted his moral rights.

Nigel Gearing is hereby identified as author of this translation of *This Child* in accordance with section 77 of the Copyright, Designs and Patents Act 1988. The author has asserted his moral rights.

Characters

PREGNANT WOMAN
MAN

FATHER
DAUGHTER (5)

FATHER (40-50)
SON (15)
WOMAN (30)

WOMAN (50)
DAUGHTER

MAN (50)
WOMAN (50)
YOUNG WOMAN WITH CHILD

MOTHER (35)
CHILD (9)

FATHER (60)
STEPMOTHER (60)
SON (30)

WOMAN IN CHILDBIRTH
VOICES

MRS MENDES
FEMALE NEIGHBOUR
POLICEMAN

MOTHER
DAUGHTER

This Child was first performed in this translation in the UK at Southwark Playhouse on 10 November 2008, directed by John Retallack and Ellen Hughes. The translation was subsequently performed on tour at The Junction Cambridge, on the 11 November 2008 directed by Jonathan Young, and at Lakeside Arts Centre on 21 November 2008 directed by Suzanne McLean Robertson.

SCENE 1

A young woman and a young man. The woman is about eight-months pregnant

PREGNANT WOMAN: At long last I'll be able to look at myself in the mirror / every morning I'll find the strength to get up / at last I'll find the strength to get a grip on my life / this child will give me strength / I'm going to show them just who I am / I'm going to show them that I'm not who they think I am / I'm going to show my parents that I'm not what they think / I'm going to show my mother that she was wrong not to believe in me / this child of mine is going to be proud to be my child / my child is going to be happy / he'll even be a child who's happier than the average child / he'll want for nothing / he won't need to beg his mother to get him something he wants / he won't even need to ask because he'll have everything he needs / everything he dreams of he'll have / because I won't let my child be sad / my child won't have a mother who's always telling him 'do you have any idea of how much that costs?' / he'll be spoiled my child / the other children will even be envious when they see how much he's spoiled / I shan't smack my child / I'll never raise a hand to my child / when he does something he shouldn't I'll explain to him quite calmly what he should do / I'll be patient / for him I'll change / I won't let myself go like I always have before / because before having my child I had no reason to be anyone out of the ordinary / I'll get a decent job with decent pay so I can become a mother who's absolutely beyond reproach / even if it's tricky to find a job I'll get up of a morning and I'll go and speak directly to those in charge/ I shan't give up / I shan't hang my head any more / on the contrary I'll look them straight in the eye till they give me what I want / I shan't give up like I used to / because now I'll have good reason to not let myself be taken advantage of / for my child

I'll become someone who does the unexpected / when I have my child I'll take care of myself / I'll take care of my body / I won't let myself go like I used to / I'll become beautiful / so he won't be ashamed / so he won't be ashamed of his mother / on the contrary so he'll be in love with his mother if it's a boy / so the other children his classmates they'll be jealous / of his having a mother who's so beautiful so feminine and so motherly at the same time / I shan't be the kind of mother whose child is sorry for her / I'll stop getting all weepy over nothing / I won't be unhappy any more / depressed / I won't be the kind of mother who's always depressed and stuck in her armchair smoking one fag after another with the TV on / one evening when I'm settled into a decent flat and when the flat's been fixed up in an impeccable way I'll invite my mother round / I'll invite my mother round so she'll realise just how wrong she was about me / I'll invite my father too even though I know he couldn't really give a toss / but I'll invite him over anyway 'cos I know that'll really mean something to my mother my father being there / my mother will realise then just who I am / she'll at last be forced to see that I can amount to something / she won't be able to *not* see it / she'll be really gutted to see what I'm capable of / what I'm capable of doing for my child / she'll be gutted to see how I'm capable of doing better than she ever did for us her children / she'll be gutted to see that my child's happy whereas we were unhappy / and she'll be gutted to see that I'm happy and that I can manage and that I'm managing and that I don't need her any more / she'll be gutted and then I'll be really happy / I'll be happy / really happy / I'll be really happy and my child will be happy too / he'll be happy / he has to be happy / he has to be.

SCENE 2

*A **FATHER** and his five-year-old **DAUGHTER**.*

FATHER: You've grown…since last time.

*Silence from the **DAUGHTER**.*

FATHER: You haven't grown?

DAUGHTER: I don't know.

FATHER: Yes you have, you're a big girl now.

DAUGHTER: I can't see it when I get bigger.

FATHER: Yes but I can.

DAUGHTER: Father, have you got bigger too?

*Silence from the **FATHER**.*

FATHER: Who are you talking to? (*Silence from the daughter.*) Who are you talking to?

DAUGHTER: I'm talking to… Father, you can see who I'm talking to. Who else is there? There's no one else here.

FATHER: So now you're calling me 'Father'?

DAUGHTER: I'm not calling you 'Father'!

FATHER: I'm your Daddy and you call me 'Father'.

DAUGHTER: Hey, am I calling you 'Father'?

FATHER: You're calling me 'Father'…how come?

DAUGHTER: I don't know… I was just asking if you, Father, had got bigger too.

FATHER: Did someone ask you to start calling me 'Father'?

DAUGHTER: No.

FATHER: You didn't use to call me 'Father'…how would you like it if I started calling you 'Daughter'?

DAUGHTER: I wouldn't mind.

FATHER: Come off it! That's no way to talk to your Daddy. (*Silence from the **DAUGHTER**.*) Does this mean you

63

don't love me, you talk to me like I'm some kind of stranger, right?

DAUGHTER: I don't know.

FATHER: Don't you want to see me any more?

DAUGHTER: I don't know.

FATHER: You don't know?

DAUGHTER: No.

FATHER: But all children need a father, right? It's like that the world over. Wouldn't you be sad if we didn't see each other again?

DAUGHTER: No.

FATHER: No? Why not?

DAUGHTER: I don't know.

FATHER: You wouldn't be sad not to see me again?

DAUGHTER: No I don't think so...

FATHER: Well, if you don't want us to see each other again, we won't see each other again, and that's that ...

DAUGHTER: Okay...

FATHER: 'Okay'? That's what you really want?

DAUGHTER: I don't mind.

FATHER: Then if it's 'okay' we won't see each other ever again...and today's the last day we'll ever see each other...if you don't want to see me ever again.

DAUGHTER: Okay.

FATHER: You're not upset?

DAUGHTER: No, because I've still got my mother...who's living in the same house as me.

FATHER: So you're saying your mother's all you need?

DAUGHTER: Yes.

FATHER: If we're never to see each other again…do you realise that today's the very last day we'll ever see each other?

DAUGHTER: Yes.

FATHER: You're not sad about that?

DAUGHTER: No.

Silence.

FATHER: Fine… I'll take you home then?

DAUGHTER: Okay.

FATHER: Straight away? That's what you want?

DAUGHTER: Sure.

FATHER: Okay I'll get my coat.

DAUGHTER: Me too.

FATHER: Yes… You're not a teeny bit sad?

DAUGHTER: No.

FATHER: You know we won't ever see each other again.

DAUGHTER: Yes I know.

FATHER: That's all you've got to say?

DAUGHTER: I don't know… it's no big deal.

FATHER: Well I'm a teeny bit sad… I'd never have imagined that one fine day such a thing could happen – a little daughter who doesn't love her Daddy.

Silence.

So we're off?

DAUGHTER: Yes that's the third time we've said so.

FATHER: I just wanted to make absolutely sure.

DAUGHTER: Sure of what?

FATHER: I don't know. (*They don't move.*) You don't see I'm sad?

DAUGHTER: No. I don't. I don't like being sad and I don't like crying.

Silence.

FATHER: Your mother will be surprised to see you back so soon.

DAUGHTER: No, she'll be pleased she'll be really pleased. She doesn't like it when I'm away from home.

SCENE 3

A flat. A man clearly in poor health, between 40 and 50. His SON, about 15. A WOMAN about 30.

FATHER: Since I gave up work I just can't feel like a real father any more.

WOMAN: But if you're not working any more it's not your fault, Mr Clough. You shouldn't go blaming yourself in this way. It's pointless.

FATHER: I just can't…a man who's not able to earn himself a living just isn't a man in my book.

WOMAN: But you're ill.

SON: It's that job of his that did for him.

WOMAN: (*To the SON.*) As far as I can tell your father isn't dead yet. Don't talk about your father like that.

SON: It's the truth. He's sweated his guts out since he was fifteen down in that hole of his. That's what's done for him. It's that shitty job of his that's fucking him over now. And – would you believe – like an arsehole he'd go right back down there again if they weren't there to stop him. Unbelievable.

WOMAN: You shouldn't talk about your father like that in front of him.

FATHER: That's how he always talks.

WOMAN: It's just not right, Mr Clough. Your son is still a child in the eyes of the law he owes you some respect.

FATHER: If truth be told the law doesn't respect me either…it forbids me to go back to work…they've taken my job away and it's the law that's responsible…for two years now I've been stuck here doing nothing, twiddling my thumbs in the flat… I get a bit tired of an evening but otherwise I feel fine… Why should they stop me from going back to work…even half-time they won't accept…truth be told, I feel I've been rather poorly treated by the law.

WOMAN: You'd like to go back to work? Back down there ? In your condition with all the pills you're on?

FATHER: Half-time at least.

SON: See how fucking stupid some people can be?

WOMAN: I've told you not to speak about your father like that.

SON: I'll say what I like. Who are you to tell me what to do?

FATHER: If you leave a man to rot like that if you leave him to stew in his corner you have no idea how that can screw him up inside. You have no idea what that can lead to inside of him. It's an absolute nightmare. A nightmare in broad daylight. Worse even: you feel you're only half a man.

WOMAN: The doctors considered you no longer fit for work… it's for your own good, Mr Clough. It's not some kind of judgement on you personally.

FATHER: Yes but I find it hard to take… You know, when it comes to being ill, I couldn't give a damn, I couldn't give a damn about what can happen to me…it's of no importance… I'm not scared…what I don't what is to rot away at home…and to feel I'm clinging on to others like some kind of parasite.

WOMAN: Why don't you get out more if you say you're feeling fine? Why don't you get out and see your friends?

A moment.

SON: He doesn't want to because he's ashamed…he's scared that his friends who are still working will take the piss out of him for being ill.

FATHER: No that's not true… I just don't want to go out, that's all.

SON: Yes it is. How many more of these arsehole excuses?

WOMAN: It's unbelievable speaking to your father like that… absolutely unbelievable…you should show some respect for your father. Don't let yourself be spoken to that like that by your own son, Mr Clough…it's unbelievable.

FATHER: He's got his own way of looking at things and I swear he didn't get it from me…everything he thinks and then all the nonsense he gets up to once he's outside the house, none of that's anything to do with what I told him. It's nothing to do with what I tell him.

SON: He'd like me to go and work like him. Go down there and work like him. Flog my guts out down some crappy hole like his, till I get sick like him and peg out at forty like him. That's what he'd like me to do. That's my father's dream, that I'll follow in his footsteps… I mean, just take a look at him. Would that make you want to lead the same kind of life as him? Honestly?

FATHER: At least you can get up of a morning and look yourself in the face.

SON: Right – the face of a corpse.

FATHER: This kid is fifteen years old and has a head full of shit.

SON: You're the one who's full of shit…you never gave a toss about me…so don't now start lecturing me on what I can and can't do.

FATHER: I'm shit even in the eyes of my son…and all because he sees his father in an armchair all day long… brooding away…instead of leading the life of a real man.

WOMAN: That still doesn't mean you should let your son get up to all kinds of nonsense outside the house, Mr Clough. It's only right I should tell you.

FATHER: He already gets up to all kinds of nonsense inside the house.

WOMAN: Do you realise that if you don't keep a tighter rein on your son, Mr Clough, they might well stop the benefits you're receiving at the moment? You can't go on letting your son run riot outside the house.

FATHER: All I'm asking is for them to let me get back to work. I don't want any benefits. I want to go back to work.

SON: He's an absolute cretin.

WOMAN: Do shut up.

FATHER: If it was up to me I'd force kids like my son to work. I'd oblige them to work. To go down the pit just so they realise what it means to learn a trade if they can't be doing with school.

SON: Hurry up and croak before anyone hears you.

FATHER: If I'd have said that to my father he'd have killed me.

SON: Yes but you're not a real man. It's you that's afraid of me 'cos you're not a man. 'Cos your life's shit and you're stuck here whining like a six-year-old all day long in your armchair... I didn't choose you. I didn't choose to have a father like you.

FATHER: I didn't choose you either. I didn't choose to have a son like you.

WOMAN: (*Exasperated.*) Okay, let's change the subject, shall we? There's no reason we shouldn't move on...

FATHER: I'm here to tell you, some evenings when he comes back my son wallops me one, how can it be that someone has so little respect for his father? How can it be? I ask myself. It's really sad.

JOËL POMMERAT

SCENE 4

*A **WOMAN** about fifty and her **DAUGHTER** (of no particular age).*

MOTHER: I'd so loved to have had a daughter who shines, shines like the sun. I did all I could, to give you an appetite for beautiful things, to be outgoing, to love light.

DAUGHTER: It's not in my nature.

MOTHER: Why not?

DAUGHTER: I don't know, Mummy.

MOTHER: You don't try.

DAUGHTER: I feel fine just as I am.

MOTHER: And other people?

DAUGHTER: What do you mean?

MOTHER: Do you think your children will enjoy growing up with that image you're giving them of their mother? (*Silence from the **DAUGHTER**.*) It's you I'm thinking of…I wouldn't like to see it all catching up with you one day. (*Silence from the **DAUGHTER**.*) I can see you have no idea of all your children could end up holding against you one day.

DAUGHTER: I don't understand.

MOTHER: I can see you don't have the first idea…

DAUGHTER: My children are fine…

MOTHER: They're children…but soon you'll become a role model for them.

DAUGHTER: There's nothing I don't do for them.

MOTHER: But you don't see how sad you are, how sad your life is. No child can live with that kind of sadness.

DAUGHTER: I'm not always sad.

MOTHER: You're dullness itself, my girl. It so upsets me to see you like this. Every day I ask myself how you could

70

have become so dismal, so lacking in spirit… Make yourself beautiful, if only for others… I'd so like you to listen to me!

DAUGHTER: I don't understand… I don't understand what you're asking me.

MOTHER: It so upsets me to see how others look on you.

DAUGHTER: I don't care.

MOTHER: Sometimes when they see the two of us together they say they can't tell who's the mother and who's the daughter. Well, they're exaggerating of course, but even so it's awful. You don't think so?

DAUGHTER: I don't care.

MOTHER: I ought to be flattered, but I'm not.

DAUGHTER: I am as I am.

MOTHER: You've really got no idea, my girl, of how things are.

DAUGHTER: No I haven't.

MOTHER: We all need a bit of brightness in our lives.

DAUGHTER: Yes.

MOTHER: Even your husband needs a bit of brightness in his life. One day or the other, you're likely to get a rude awakening.

DAUGHTER: What do you mean?

MOTHER: Try and see the world for what it really is, my girl, it's important.

DAUGHTER: I don't understand.

MOTHER: No you don't understand, I can see that.

DAUGHTER: What do you mean?

MOTHER: See the look your husband gives out, then you'll understand.

DAUGHTER: ?

MOTHER: It's 'cos of you.

DAUGHTER: I know, Mummy, but I don't understand.

MOTHER: You should take note of the look your husband gives out when he's with you, well, I for one find it upsetting, it upsets me enormously, in the first place 'cos it's your husband, and then 'cos he could be my son.

DAUGHTER: What's this look you see him giving out?

MOTHER: Do you want me to spell it out?

DAUGHTER: I don't understand…

MOTHER: I'm sorry for you, my girl, but it's all horribly predictable, alas all too horribly predictable.

DAUGHTER: I know my husband cares for me.

MOTHER: I'm so sad for you, that even this much you can't understand, I'm so sad.

DAUGHTER: No really I don't understand.

MOTHER: If you only knew what a difficult time ahead you're storing up for yourself, my girl… And yet I've done all I could for you, truly I have. I don't think I'm to blame. I've done all I could for you to love light, for you to be bright and shiny as the sun. I've done all I could. I've done all I could to give you an appetite for beautiful things, to make you want to shine, to look your best, to be really outgoing, above all to love light.

DAUGHTER: I'm sorry, Mummy, but I've always done my very best, always my very best.

SCENE 5

In a block of flats. On the doorstep of one particular flat. A gentle-looking couple in their 50s and a **YOUNG WOMAN WITH A CHILD** *a few weeks old in her arms.*

YOUNG WOMAN WITH CHILD: You don't have any children?

WOMAN: No.

YWWC: When I pass you on the stairs, each time I pass you, I see you looking at the baby in such a way I think you must really like children.

WOMAN: Yes, we like children a lot.

YWWC: We've never really met we just pass each other on the stairs.

WOMAN: Yes, that's right.

YWWC: You've never had children?

WOMAN: No.

YWWC: But you look as if you like children...

WOMAN: Yes. A lot.

YWWC: But you've never had children?

WOMAN: No.

YWWC: Isn't that a bit sad?

WOMAN: No, it's fine.

YWWC: Because you couldn't?

MAN: That's right.

YWWC: Isn't that a bit sad?

MAN: Yes, a bit but it's fine.

YWWC: Each time we pass on the stairs I notice your eyes when you look at the baby...

WOMAN: He's such a lovely baby.

YWWC: We pass on the stairs practically every day and yet we've never really got to know each other.

MAN: No we haven't.

YWWC: You didn't try to adopt?

WOMAN: How do you mean?

YWWC: A child, a baby.

WOMAN: We tried.

YWWC: You tried.

MAN: Yes.

YWWC: It's a shame it didn't work out.

MAN: Yes but you know…it's not something we think about every day.

YWWC: Every time we pass on the stairs I see you look at the baby in such a way.

MAN: Really?

WOMAN: I told my husband. Don't look at the baby like that. You'll upset the lady, it could be upsetting.

YWWC: You know, it doesn't upset me, in fact I rather like it.

WOMAN: Well good.

YWWC: (*Going up to the WOMAN with her child.*) Here.

MAN: Yes?

YWWC: Here, take him if you like.

She plumps the child in the arms of the MAN.

MAN: Yes just for a moment.

The MAN and the WOMAN, very moved, look at the baby.

WOMAN: He's so tiny!

MAN: They're so tiny at that age.

WOMAN: (*Tenderly, to her HUSBAND.*) It's a bit silly to say that.

MAN: I mean I've never held a baby of this age before.

WOMAN: Yes.

YWWC: I'm giving him to you.

MAN & WOMAN: What?

YWWC: I'm giving him to you, he's yours now.

MAN: Excuse me?

YWWC: I'm giving him to you I've given it a lot of thought.

WOMAN: What are you saying?

YWWC: I'm giving him to you he's yours.

MAN: How can you say such a thing?

YWWC: I feel good you know I'm really very well… I feel really good… I've been seeing you for some months now round the building… I pass you every day you look so happy together the two of you…you look so open with people, so obviously easygoing with everyone…so considerate and attentive, caring even…with children but not only with them… I see you like that with everybody.

MAN: This is unreal.

YWWC: Don't be frightened it's all very simple.

WOMAN: You're not serious?

YWWC: Yes I am. Absolutely… I'm telling you I'm giving you this child… I'm perfectly fine…don't be frightened. I love this child… I really love him and I really want him to be happy .. That's why I'm giving him to you… You see I'm still young I could have more children one day…but for the time being I'm giving you this one.

MAN: This just isn't possible.

YWWC: Yes it's perfectly possible and perfectly serious on my part…and I've given it my fullest consideration as well.

MAN: Well of course we can't possibly accept.

YWWC: Why ever not? Of course you can! I'm giving him to you: he's yours… How can you seriously suggest he'd be unhappy with you? You have so much love, I know,I feel you have love in you… I'd never give away my child just like that…into the care of just anyone… Never… I'd rather die first…but in this case, well… I know this child will be happy…very very happy. (*Silence.*) You don't want children? You don't dream of it? Won't your life have been a miserable failure without children? What could be more wonderful in life?

WOMAN: But we can't… It's just not done…not like this at any rate.

YWWC: Then how?

MAN: What about you?

YWWC: Me?

MAN: Yes.

YWWC: With me he can't be really happy…totally happy it's impossible I know, I can see.

MAN: You shouldn't say that.

YWWC: That's 'cos you don't know me… You don't know what goes on in my head…all the heavy stuff I carry round in my head… I still can't manage to live… really…for myself… Right? I still can't manage to get up of a morning… I still can't manage to go to bed at night…I still can't manage to go to a supermarket to do the shopping… I still can't manage to fill in the forms to get benefits although I've got no money… When I look at myself in the mirror, I still can't manage to feel like a real mother. Right? When I see you two I know you are parent-material. When I see myself I know I'm not a mother… I love this child… I really do. I'd so love him to be happy, I'd so love him to be given love. Don't imagine that I don't love this child I love him so much I love him, you know, but I don't love him as a mother, no that's something I feel I know inside of me, I don't love him as a mother should love her child I feel love for him but another different kind of love…that's why I can contemplate living away from him you know providing I know he's happy…do you understand? (*Silence.*) I know that with you he'll be happy…that's the most important thing…you understand? That's why I'm giving him to you…there you are… I'll be off now…so… I'll go and fetch his things… I'll be right back and then I'll be off, I'll leave him with you… That's what we'll do.

She goes off. The couple, stunned, remain there with the child in their arms.

SCENE 6

A flat. A 35-year-old woman seated on the sofa. TV on in a corner.

CHILD: Did you call me, Mummy?

MOTHER: Yes.

CHILD: What do you want?

MOTHER: Nothing. I just wanted to see you for a bit. You're always in your room.

CHILD: I'm in a hurry, Mummy. I don't want to be late for school again today.

MOTHER: You've never been told off for being late to school.

CHILD: Never. But I don't like it. Being late. It upsets me.

MOTHER: You're late because you dawdle.

CHILD: No, Mummy. I'm late 'cos you always want to talk to me just as I'm leaving.

MOTHER: (*Gently.*) How rude you've become with me!

CHILD: Sorry, Mummy, but it's the truth. I'm telling the truth. I don't mean to be rude, Mummy. Not to you.

MOTHER: (*Gently.*) How is it you've become so rude? What's happened? Or not happened? For you to become like this…with your own mother…you're not yet ten …

CHILD: Sorry, Mummy, I didn't mean to upset you… I just wanted you to realise something that means a lot to me: I don't like being late for school… I really don't like it …

MOTHER: Take your coat off. I've told you before…indoors.

CHILD: I'm about to go out, Mummy.

MOTHER: It's all of three minutes between here and school. What are you talking about?

CHILD: I like getting to school a bit early. I told you before, it makes me feel better.

MOTHER: The other children aren't like this. Why are you like this?

CHILD: I don't know, Mummy.

MOTHER: Is it my fault? Is that what you mean?

CHILD: No, Mummy, it's not your fault. You do the best you can. I know that.

MOTHER: Yes even though I believe I do everything I can...and you know that...'cos you see that.

CHILD: Yes I know I see that.

MOTHER: Even though I really make an effort, even though I do all I can. Even though my situation is really not that easy, and you know that. I think you could be just a little more understanding.

CHILD: Mummy, I try to be understanding.

MOTHER: Yes, I know, I'm sorry.

CHILD: No , Mummy. It's me who should be sorry. I know your situation isn't easy.

MOTHER: I'm not a good mother, I shouldn't make you share my problems... I ought to be able to deal with them all by myself... I should be able to cope with more than I do. That's what a good mother's all about.

CHILD: No, Mummy, I told you before I don't want you to bottle up things inside... I don't want that...in fact I want you to confide in me...and for us to sort out problems together.

MOTHER: No, it's not your job to sort out my problems.

CHILD: I told you before to stop talking like this... I'm not three any more, I'm ten, I'm a man, I can perfectly well understand your problems... I'm strong enough to help you deal with your problems.

MOTHER: How lucky I am to have a son like you…how lucky I am to have a boy like you.

CHILD: Yes, Mummy, don't be frightened…you shouldn't be frightened, I don't like it when you're frightened, it upsets me I get all nervy and irritable…at school I get so I can't stand the others… I become aggressive the moment someone is nasty to me… I want to hit them…in fact sometimes I do… I don't always manage to stop myself.

MOTHER: You shouldn't get into fights.

CHILD: Yes I know.

MOTHER: It make me unhappy knowing you can be violent.

CHILD: Yes. Sorry, Mummy.

MOTHER: Come closer, come a little closer, please, take your coat off, I already told you.

CHILD: I have to go…this time I'm not early…if I don't leave now I'll be late even…

MOTHER: Don't go on so… You're top of the school you're top of all the pupils in your class… I'm proud of you…so you have the right not to be on time every single day… I have the right to give you a hug after all…a mother has the right to give her child a hug.

CHILD: Yes, Mummy.

MOTHER: I need you to give me a bit of a hug… I need it… there's more than just talking to me like you do…you know I've found you a bit distant just recently…you've become distant you don't hug me to you any more you no longer call me your little mummy darling – you don't kiss me as much as you used to…it's almost as if you were avoiding me…when it comes to discussing things yes you're very good but when it comes to other things it's like you're trying to run away from me .

CHILD: Hey – look! I'm late…

MOTHER: You're running away from me! Oh my God, what have I done to have a son whose only thought is to be always running away from me, always escaping me?

CHILD: I'm sorry, Mummy.

MOTHER: Then go! Leave! Go and find your friends at school. Your school-mistress who so adores you, who seems to worship the ground you walk on! Go! I just hope you won't come to regret it!

CHILD: What do you mean?

MOTHER: I don't know… I don't know any more… Just once in a while you could not go to school, skip school and stay home.

CHILD: But it's very serious if I skip school. I mustn't.

MOTHER: Sadly, worse things could happen, you know. A lot worse.

Silence.

SCENE 7

*A flat. A **FATHER**, just over 60, his **SON** aged 30, and his **WIFE** the same age.*

FATHER: All I'm trying to say is that children need to be dealt with more strictly, especially on the father's side…that's all I'm trying to say… I think you're too easy-going with your son… I don't think it's right for children to rule the roost like that, especially with their father.

SON: I don't want to talk about it, Dad.

STEPMOTHER: (*To SON.*) Why don't you want to talk about it… you might at least listen to your father when he has something to say, the poor bugger.

SON: No, I'm sorry, I don't want to.

FATHER: Why do you close yourself off like this.

SON: I don't know.

FATHER: It's a shame you don't want to talk about it…

SON: Yes, well, that's how it is.

FATHER: It's a shame because I think it's really important for your son that you don't allow him to do everything he's a mind to all the time…that you don't let him do whatever he fancies.

SON: I don't let him do whatever he fancies.

FATHER: That's not how it looks to me…it looks to me like he's the one ordering you around in your own home I've never seen a child speak so rudely to his father…in his own home.

SON: Shut up, Dad.

FATHER: If you'd ever spoken to me like your son speaks to you you'd have lived to regret it…you'd never have spoken to me like that…you'd never have dared…and God knows you weren't the easiest of kids…

SON: Shut up please, Dad.

FATHER: What's more, I'd like to point out it could all have ended very badly for you…just as it could have ended very badly for me too if my father hadn't kept a tight rein on me, it was no joke putting up with it day in day out I saw the back of his hand as well, anything he found to hand was good enough for him but at least it stopped me from getting up to all manner of things and now I thank him for it. You know if you let a child do just what it wants you're doing him no favours, you're doing no favours to anyone to let a child just do what it wants…on the contrary it's a recipe for disaster…it's the end of all respect and authority…it's a recipe for disaster.

SON: Stop, Dad, shut up, please.

FATHER: It's no more than the truth…but you weren't the easiest of children on the contrary you were a difficult child just as I was in my time…just like your son now

and I know if I hadn't played it by my rules you'd
have played it by yours one day and that's for sure.

SON: Shut up, d'you hear?

FATHER: You might not want to talk about it but there's no
denying it...if today you have the life you have – a
fine peaceful decent life with a wife as nice and as
beautiful as yours –

SON: (*On the point of exploding.*) Shut up, for Christ's sake.

FATHER: If today you have this orderly peaceful life I flatter
myself that I have something to do with it.

SON: (*Barely holding back.*) Shut up.

FATHER: You don't want to talk about it... You're afraid to talk
about it, anyone might think you're afraid to.

SON: (*No longer able to hold back.*) Shut up!

FATHER: Okay I'll shut up I see you don't want to listen to me
and you don't want to talk.

SON: (*Exploding.*) Please... I don't want to talk to you...
especially...don't get me to say what's on my mind,
please...you're so proud of how you were brought
up...you're so proud of your set of rules, which
you managed to impose on me...you're so proud of
how strong you are...you're so proud of the result.
(*He gets up.*) Take a look at just how proud you
can be of the result... Look at me, yes, you can
be proud, you brought me up as you should...you
brought me up properly, you never had cause for
complaint when it came to me... I never interrupted
you at the dinner-table... I never showed you
disrespect when guests were around... I never said
as much as a word when you were there unless
you gave me permission to do so...not even when
it was just us the family...even nowadays you have
no idea how difficult it is for me to talk to you...to
dare to talk to you... Because I was always
frightened of you even without you needing to

raise your voice… You terrorised me all my childhood, all my adolescence, all my youth… Yes, you might well be proud… I was frightened of you just like a child should be frightened of its father according to you…and even now when you're there in a corner in your chair all day long…and when you can scarcely be heard because you always speak so softly like you were afraid of interrupting something…too right I'm afraid, I'm still frightened of you, still trembling inside… I'm afraid of you…the moment you come into the same room as me…the moment you come near me…the moment you say something to me, I start to feel unwell I start feeling sick inside, I feel this real fear rising up inside me… I can't help it. I'd so love to be rid of this fear…this fear which drains me, exhausts me, destroys me…If I seem aggressive most of the time I know full well it's to cover up this fear…but I'd so love to get over this aggressiveness, this aggressiveness with others and with myself… I'd so love, I'd so love to spare my son that fear… I'd so love to spare him that… I'd so love my son to be able to look at me without feeling that fear, without trembling…

I'd so love to be able to come up to my son without seeing the anxiety and the fear in his look… Sorry, Dad, but I'd so love to be there for my son in ways you couldn't be for me… I'd so love for my son to feel towards me something other than what I feel towards you… I'd so love I'd so love that, if it were at all possible… Sorry, I'd so love to be different from you…

He goes out. The **FATHER** *and* **STEPMOTHER** *remain. Silent.*

SCENE 8

Total darkness. A woman's silhouette. Around her male and female voices.

VOICES:

- But you're not pushing.
- You're holding the child back, love.
- You're afraid.
- She's holding it back.
- You shouldn't be afraid.

WOMAN'S VOICE: But I'm not afraid.

A VOICE: The child wants to come out.

WOMAN'S VOICE: I want it to come out.

VOICES:

- You can shout don't be afraid to shout you can shout.
- Help us, love.

WOMAN'S VOICE: Help me.

VOICES:

- What do you think we're doing?
- You're not relaxed.
- You're not relaxing.
- Don't be afraid to shout.
- She shouts often enough.

WOMAN'S VOICE: I want it to come out.

A VOICE: But you're keeping it in.

WOMAN'S VOICE: I want it to come out.

VOICES:

- Don't hold it back.
- She's tired.
- But the child isn't coming out.
- She's holding the child back.
- Don't hold it back, love.

WOMAN'S VOICE: I want it to come out.

VOICES:
> – The child wants to come out, love.
> – Push.
> – Make him come out.
> – You don't want him to come out.
> – Push.
> – Stop shouting and just push.

WOMAN'S VOICE: I am pushing.

VOICES:
> – Breathe!
> – The child is coming but you're holding it back.
> – Why won't he come out?
> – She's holding it back.
> – Where's the father?
> – There is no father. There never has been.
> – There was a man here a while ago.
> – That wasn't the father.
> – It was a man.
> – Don't hold your child back, love.

WOMAN'S VOICE: I want it to come out.

VOICES:
> – You're holding your child back.
> – You can't keep it in there any longer.

WOMAN'S VOICE: I don't want to keep it any longer.

A VOICE: So push.

WOMAN'S VOICE: I'm frightened it doesn't want to come out.

A VOICE: It's you who's holding it back.

WOMAN'S VOICE: I get the feeling he's afraid.

A VOICE: You're the one who's afraid.

ANOTHER VOICE: We need to get this over with now.

SCENE 9[1]

*A room in a hospital. In that room: a body under
a white sheet. Two women and a man in the
doorway.*

MRS MENDES: She's a friend, she's my neighbour she came with me.

POLICEMAN: She can't come in with you.

MRS MENDES: She can't come in with me?

POLICEMAN: No she can't.

NEIGHBOUR: It doesn't matter I'll wait here.

POLICEMAN: Only family can come in.

MRS MENDES: (*Gesturing to the body placed under the white
sheet.*) I'm not family to whoever's there either… it's
not my son after all, it can't be my son.

NEIGHBOUR: Go ahead, that way you'll know once and for all.

POLICEMAN: So I'm asking you to confirm for us that this is not
your son…

MRS MENDES: But since after all it's not my son…

NEIGHBOUR: Go ahead anyway.

MRS MENDES: I don't want to.

NEIGHBOUR: What have you got to lose?

MRS MENDES: I don't want to.

POLICEMAN: You just lift up the sheet, you look under the sheet…
and then, since it's not your son after all, you simply
say to me it's not my son.

MRS MENDES: I don't want to look under the sheet.

POLICEMAN: What have you got to lose, Ma'am.

NEIGHBOUR: Go ahead, you know I'm here.

MRS MENDES: Yes.

NEIGHBOUR: Go ahead, it's stupid, it's just a formality.

---

1   *Suggested by a scene from* Jackets *by Edward Bond*

MRS MENDES: Yes, you're right.

POLICEMAN: Go ahead, Ma'am.

MRS MENDES: But it's silly, I know full well it can't be him, but now I'm frightened.

NEIGHBOUR: But it's ridiculous, you know that.

MRS MENDES: Yes.

NEIGHBOUR: You said yourself you know full well where your son is at the moment, he can't be contacted, okay, but you know perfectly well where he is and what he's doing at the moment.

MRS MENDES: He's off camping.

NEIGHBOUR: He's off camping with my son and three other morons of their age…a right old laugh they'd have if they could see us now.

MRS MENDES: You're telling me …

NEIGHBOUR: (*To the POLICEMAN.*) They never stop making fun of us for worrying over nothing whatsoever…we get on their nerves, it's true sometimes we really mollycoddle them.

MRS MENDES: What d'you expect? We love our sons.

NEIGHBOUR: They're all we've got – besides, their fathers have buggered off. (*To POLICEMAN.*) You've got kids too?

MRS MENDES: Wait. Okay. I'll do it.

NEIGHBOUR: Show me a father who hasn't buggered off.

POLICEMAN: Go ahead, Ma'am.

MRS MENDES: Yes, I'll do it, what have I got to lose.

NEIGHBOUR: Yes, that's right and then we can leave.

MRS MENDES: I'll do it .(*Silence. She goes.*) What have I got to lose.

NEIGHBOUR: Nothing.

MRS MENDES: (*Moving closer to the body under the sheet.*) At least that way I'll know once and for all.

NEIGHBOUR: And that way we can leave and go home.

MRS MENDES: I'll invite you in. We'll flop out on the sofa. And we'll wait in peace and quiet. We'll wait in peace and quiet, we'll wait for our children to come back.

She stops. She turns back to her friend. As if she was going to go no further.

NEIGHBOUR: Go ahead. You know perfectly well that it can't be your kid.

MRS MENDES: I really don't see how it could be.

NEIGHBOUR: It's a body they found a couple of hundred yards from the house, on a building site where dropouts hang about and get off their heads morning noon and night… what's that got to do with your son?…your son is a hundred miles away, in the countryside… come off it.

MRS MENDES: My son's gone camping.

NEIGHBOUR: Your son's gone camping.

MRS MENDES: With yours.

NEIGHBOUR: Yes with mine. They're off camping, the two of them, with pals.

MRS MENDES: So why should someone round our way see the body and say Heavens, that looks like Mrs Mendes' kid?

NEIGHBOUR: They didn't say Heavens, that looks like Mrs Mendes' kid, they said that looks like the same light-blue top that Mrs Mendes' son wears.

MRS MENDES: (*Gesturing to the body.*) You can't see his top there.

NEIGHBOUR: Your kid's not the only kid round here to have a light-blue top, half the kids round here wear one.

MRS MENDES: They're so unattractive.

NEIGHBOUR: You know that our kids like what's unattractive.

MRS MENDES: I'll say.

POLICEMAN: It's just a routine verification, ladies.

NEIGHBOUR: Yes, go ahead.

MRS MENDES: I'll do it. No, I can't.

NEIGHBOUR: Why not?

MRS MENDES: I don't know. Or rather I do.

NEIGHBOUR: What do you mean?

MRS MENDES: What if it was him?

NEIGHBOUR: Hey, come off it.

MRS MENDES: It's him… I feel it's him… Now I get the feeling it's him. It's him. It's him.

NEIGHBOUR: Come off it.

MRS MENDES: I'm sure it's him.

NEIGHBOUR: Stop this at once. Don't get hysterical. Are you listening to me, Elisabeth?!

POLICEMAN: Just verify for us, Ma'am, like that it'll all be much simpler.

NEIGHBOUR: Go ahead, Elisabeth. That way imagine how relieved you'll be. I'm telling you it's not him. It's not your son.

MRS MENDES: You think so?

NEIGHBOUR: Why else would I say so?

MRS MENDES: Yes of course…you're right.

NEIGHBOUR: Go on, go ahead, don't hang around.

MRS MENDES: I'll do it.

She steps forward.

POLICEMAN: Just lift up the sheet, Ma'am. And then it's all over.

MRS MENDES: (*Next to the body under the sheet.*) Okay. Right. Here goes…

POLICEMAN: You just lift it up.

NEIGHBOUR: You lift it up.

POLICEMAN: You lift up the sheet.

NEIGHBOUR: Go on, go ahead, just lift up the sheet, for God's sake, it's unbelievable, what are you playing at.

MRS MENDES: (*Still not lifting up the sheet.*) It's him.

NEIGHBOUR: For Christ's sake. It's not true. You're a real pain in the neck, it's not true. Take hold of the sheet and just lift it up. I'm telling you it's not your son it can't be your son.

MRS MENDES: Yes. Right.

> *Silence.*

> *She takes hold of the sheet. She shuts her eyes. Eyes still shut, head raised, she lifts up the sheet. The sheet is now lifted up. She opens her eyes. A moment. She has her eyes open, without looking. Then she lowers her head. She looks, she puts the sheet back.*

MRS MENDES: It's not my son.

NEIGHBOUR: You see? What did I tell you? You have no idea how much you scared the shit out of me.

MRS MENDES: It's not my son it's not my son it's not my son it's not my son it's not my son.

NEIGHBOUR: You see! What did I say? You're a real pain in the neck, you should listen to others a bit more.

MRS MENDES: It's not my son it's not my son it's not my son it's not my son it's not my son it's not my son.

NEIGHBOUR: I'm knackered…this whole business has left me completely knackered. (*MRS MENDES starts to laugh hysterically – clearly a nervous reaction.*) I'd rather see you like this if I'm being honest. If I'm being honest I'd glad to see you like this. (*MRS MENDES continues to laugh hysterically.*) Look at her now, laughing like she's mental… (*MRS MENDES's laughter is contagious.*) Hey, that's it, we can leave now, right?

> *MRS MENDES carries on laughing. Still stands there beside the corpse. More laughter…*

NEIGHBOUR: (*Also laughing but less heartily.*) It's not true, hey, enough of this. Come on – we're leaving. We're getting out of here… Come on… It's not really the right place for this. (***MRS MENDES*** *is laughing even more.*) Elisabeth, come on, we're leaving. (*Laughter.*) Come on: listen to me. (*Laughter.*) No, listen – this isn't real. (***MRS MENDES*** *suddenly stops laughing. Silence.*) What's wrong?

MRS MENDES: I know…that face …

NEIGHBOUR: What?

MRS MENDES: I recognise it!

NEIGHBOUR: What are you saying?

MRS MENDES: I think I recognise that face.

NEIGHBOUR: You know who it is?

MRS MENDES: That face – it's a face I recognise. I think I know that face.

NEIGHBOUR: You recognise it?

MRS MENDES: Yes…that face. That face… I know it. I know that face very well… Oh! My God it's not true…

NEIGHBOUR: Elisabeth, are you winding us up?… What's going on?

MRS MENDES: Yes…of course I do… Oh my God it's not true! Yes.

NEIGHBOUR: Then tell us for God's sake, who is it?

MRS MENDES: It's my.

NEIGHBOUR: It's your.

MRS MENDES: That face – it's my son. (*Silence from the neighbour.*) It's my son…why should that face…? Why should that face mean something like it does if it wasn't my son? It's him…it's my son… It's him…it's my son… I didn't want to see it was my son…but it's my son …

NEIGHBOUR: Oh no – fuck – it can't be true!

MRS MENDES: Help me. Please.

POLICEMAN: Take a good look, Ma'am. Lift up the sheet again.

MRS MENDES: Never again – I couldn't.

POLICEMAN: Lift up the sheet, Ma'am.

MRS MENDES: No, I can't.

NEIGHBOUR: Do you have a chair somewhere here, I'd like to sit down.

MRS MENDES: It's my son! I knew that one day something like this would happen to me… I just knew it. When I split up with his father. I felt it. That I'd pay for it… One day. Inevitably – one day – that I'd have to pay for it… Poor kids. It's awful for them having parents like us unable to love each other. Our children pay a heavy price. They pay for it. My son's paying… My God… my son's paying for all my mistakes… Oh my God.

NEIGHBOUR: Shut up, Elisabeth!

MRS MENDES: I'm a criminal. All the women who've split up with their husbands are criminals. We've killed our children. I've killed my child… Now my child's dead, I've killed him.

NEIGHBOUR: You're off your head. Calm down. Lift up the sheet again. Please.

MRS MENDES: No I can't.

NEIGHBOUR: Are you really sure about what you're saying? Are you certain about what you saw? Before you said it wasn't him?

MRS MENDES: Now I know it was him!

NEIGHBOUR: Take another look. If it had been him you'd have seen straight away. You'd have seen it was him… You couldn't have not seen him when you lifted the sheet up, you couldn't have been mistaken like that …

MRS MENDES: I didn't want to see him – that's why.

NEIGHBOUR: This is all too much, Elisabeth… I don't know what to do to help you.

MRS MENDES: You're going to have to help me through it, I don't know what'll become of me.

POLICEMAN: Look again, Ma'am.

MRS MENDES: Stop telling me what I should do!

NEIGHBOUR: Calm down, Elisabeth.

MRS MENDES: I've killed my child.

NEIGHBOUR: You have not killed your child, Elisabeth.

MRS MENDES: I brought my child into this world and then I killed him the day I left his father.

NEIGHBOUR: That's enough! Pull yourself together and lift up the sheet!

MRS MENDES: I know it's my son that's there under that sheet.

NEIGHBOUR: Lift up the sheet again.

> *MRS MENDES abruptly falls to her knees.*

MRS MENDES: I'm lifting the sheet, right?

> *She doesn't lift the sheet. A moment. Then she does. Exposes the body. Looks. Then puts the sheet back in place. Silence.*

NEIGHBOUR: Elisabeth? (*Silence from MRS MENDES.*) Say something!

MRS MENDES: It's not him.

NEIGHBOUR: What did I tell you? You're a real pain… I'm knackered…you scared the living daylights out of me.

MRS MENDES: It's not him.

NEIGHBOUR: What have I been telling you?… Really, you piss me off.

MRS MENDES: It's not my son.

NEIGHBOUR: Your child is fast asleep, Heaven knows where…

MRS MENDES: It's not my son…

NEIGHBOUR: …or frying up potatoes over a fire…with my kid outside their tent.

MRS MENDES: Thank God. Thank God.

NEIGHBOUR: What's he got to do with your son – some poor little sod hanging out in some building-site where they're shooting up all the time.

MRS MENDES: My God, I'm so happy, I've never felt like this before, it's horrible.

NEIGHBOUR: You wind yourself up! Come on, we're leaving now, I want to leave now, I'll never forget what a hard time you've given me.

MRS MENDES: Oh my God, thank you, thank you God.

NEIGHBOUR: Okay come on, let's go now please, Elisabeth… let's leave these people to finish their job. (*MRS MENDES starts to laugh again.*) Come now, please, I've had enough of this now, I'm beat.

MRS MENDES laughs.

POLICEMAN: Ma'am, if it's not your child, you can leave now.

MRS MENDES laughs.

NEIGHBOUR: Come on, Elisabeth, let's leave.

MRS MENDES laughs.

POLICEMAN: Come on, Ma'am.

While still continuing to laugh MRS MENDES signals to the policeman for him to come over to her.

NEIGHBOUR: What now?

She laughs and signals to the policeman.

POLICEMAN: You have to leave now, Ma'am.

She carries on signalling.

NEIGHBOUR: Go ahead. It's like she wants to say something.

MRS MENDES: (*Unable to stop laughing.*) Please! (*She carries on laughing.*) Oh no!

POLICEMAN: What's going on, Ma'am? (*He moves over to MRS MENDES.*) You can't stay here…now.

MRS MENDES: (*Unable to stop her laughing fit.*) Oh no, my God, it really hurts!

POLICEMAN: You can't stay here!

NEIGHBOUR: What's going on, Elisabeth?

MRS MENDES: (*Aside to the **POLICEMAN**.*) I'm so happy, I've never been so happy, it's terrible. It's not my son, if you had any idea how happy I am, I was so frightened, I was so convinced it was him, I was so certain.

POLICEMAN: You must leave, Ma'am.

MRS MENDES: (*Aside to the **POLICEMAN**.*) I'm so happy you can't imagine, it's terrible but I'm so happy.

POLICEMAN: Please, Ma'am, you can't stay here.

NEIGHBOUR: What's going on, Elisabeth? What are you playing at?

POLICEMAN: Go and be with your friend, Ma'am.

NEIGHBOUR: (*Aside to the **POLICEMAN**.*) It's not her son, what a little prick he is, what an earful he's going to get when he gets home.

POLICEMAN: Go ahead.

MRS MENDES: It's not my son, I'm so happy.

POLICEMAN: This way.

MRS MENDES: No I can't…

NEIGHBOUR: What's going on?

MRS MENDES: I don't want to be with her …

POLICEMAN: What's going on, Ma'am?

NEIGHBOUR: What's going on, Elisabeth?

MRS MENDES: (*Laughing.*) Oh please God.

NEIGHBOUR: What are you doing?

MRS MENDES: (*Aside to the **POLICEMAN**.*) It's awful I'm so happy, it's so dreadful, I'm so happy it's like I'm crazy, it's dreadful I was so frightened that's why…but it's her son, her son, it's awful, ghastly, dreadful, I know, it's her son, her son but you can't imagine how happy I am, how happy I am that it's not mine, that it's not my son but hers...do you understand?

*No reply from the **POLICEMAN**.*

NEIGHBOUR: What's going on?

MRS MENDES: (*Aside to **POLICEMAN**.*) For God's sake, you tell her...it's so awful and I'm so happy.

NEIGHBOUR: What are you doing? Elisabeth, I'm leaving now!

MRS MENDES: (*Laughing.*) Oh my God, it's awful, but I'm so happy! It's awful it's awful it's awful.

Silence.

NEIGHBOUR: (*Looking worried.*) What's going on?

POLICEMAN: (*Turning to the **NEIGHBOUR**.*) Ma'am, I'm sorry, would you mind stepping forward...and coming over here.

NEIGHBOUR: Whatever for?

POLICEMAN: Would you mind telling us if you recognise the person lying under the sheet?

NEIGHBOUR: I don't understand.

POLICEMAN: It's possible, Ma'am, that you know whoever's under that sheet.

NEIGHBOUR: Since it's not my son, I don't see how...I don't see how me, I personally could know whoever's ...

POLICEMAN: Just step over here and then lift up the sheet, Ma'am...

NEIGHBOUR: I don't want to.

POLICEMAN: I'm simply asking you to confirm for us that you don't know whoever's under the sheet.

NEIGHBOUR: No I shan't, I don't want to.

POLICEMAN: Please, Ma'am.

MRS MENDES: I'm so happy it's awful to be as happy as I am now.

SCENE 10

*A **MOTHER** and her **DAUGHTER**. A flat. The daughter
is alone. Seated. The **MOTHER** enters from behind.
She says nothing.*

DAUGHTER: Why have you come to see me? I told you that I didn't
want to see you outside of those days you come to
see your grandchildren.

MOTHER: You're so mean. Why are you being so mean?

DAUGHTER: You tell me, Mummy. Why do you think I'm being so
mean?

MOTHER: I don't know. I don't understand…

DAUGHTER: You don't know.

MOTHER: No. Can I come in?

DAUGHTER: No.

MOTHER: You're so mean. I feel sorry for you. My poor girl – you
must be very unhappy. (*Silence.*) Well I'll be off then.
Goodbye, Daughter.

DAUGHTER: Goodbye, Mother.

MOTHER: You're so mean. I don't understand you. I'm sorry for
you.

*The **MOTHER** leaves. Comes back.*

I haven't gone yet.

DAUGHTER: So I see.

MOTHER: I just wanted to say…

DAUGHTER: What do you still want to say to me, Mummy?

MOTHER: I wanted to tell you…that it isn't true …

DAUGHTER: What isn't true?

MOTHER: It isn't true that I don't understand you…it isn't true
that you're mean…you're not really mean …

DAUGHTER: You don't say.

MOTHER: No you're not mean. That's not being mean, my
girl. No. That's not it. Being mean is something else
altogether. Being mean is something else again.
Being mean. I'm going to tell you. It's very simple.
Very simple to tell you. Because it's precisely how
I've been. How I've been myself, how I've been
myself with you. Now that's a perfect example of
how to be mean. Of someone being mean. Oh yes.
Oh yes there you'd be on to something. There you'd
be within your rights to say I've been mean. You'd
be the one to say I've been mean. Because it's the
truth, child. I've been very mean. I've been mean.
I've been mean. You you're not mean to me. You
never say anything wounding or nasty. Never. It's true
you tell me that you don't want to see me. But that's
really to be expected. That's really to be expected. If
you only knew how deeply I understand you… After
all… After all you've had to put up with. Put up with
from your mother. If you only knew how fortunate
I consider myself. How fortunate I consider myself
that you hold back…that you hold back from venting
all your anger at me, all your resentment, all those
words you have bottled up inside of you and which
could annihilate me. If you only knew how deeply I
understand you, how I understand your anger your
resentment towards me, and how grateful I am to
you how grateful I am to you for your goodness, for
your attitude towards me which makes you keep
inside of you all those words all that anger towards
me. Yes quite sincerely, I'm grateful, my girl, for your
generosity of spirit, something I never had when it
came to you, something you never got from me and
yet you managed to cultivate inside of you, yes you're
the one to teach me something, I'm the one who's
learned from you, my girl, and I thank you for it. You
know a mother can learn a lot from her children. I'd
have so loved to realise that earlier than I did. I'd have
so loved to realise that you can't know all there is to
know, that you don't have to know all there is to know

straight off… I'm telling you I'm sorry, my girl, truly I am, I'm asking you to forgive me for not being the mother you deserved to have… Sorry… I'll go now.

*The **MOTHER** goes off.*

DAUGHTER: Yes, Mummy. Thanks. Go now.

END OF PLAY

RESPECT

By Lutz Hübner

Translated by Zoë Svendsen

Further Copyright Information

Respect / Ehrensache

Lutz Hübner is hereby identified as author of *Respect* in accordance with section 77 of the Copyright, Designs and Patents Act 1988. The author has asserted his moral rights.

Zoë Svendsen is hereby identified as translator of *Respect* in accordance with section 77 of the Copyright, Designs and Patents Act 1988. The author has asserted her moral rights.

Characters

CEM
19 YEARS OLD, AN APPRENTICE

SINAN
17 YEARS OLD, AT SCHOOL

ELENA
16 YEARS OLD, AT SCHOOL

ULLI
15 YEARS OLD, AT SCHOOL

KOBERT
30 YEARS OLD, POLICE PSYCHOLOGIST

Staging
The stage is divided into three levels:

*The conversations between **CEM** or **SINAN** with **KOBERT***

***ULLI**'s monologues*

The flashbacks

The levels must be divided such that in the final scene the different levels can merge. The stage should be as bare as possible, just with minimal props to indicate the different places in which the flashbacks occur.

Time
Period leading up to the trial, with flashbacks to the day the crime took place.

SCENE 1

KOBERT, CEM.

KOBERT: My name's Kobert.

CEM nods.

KOBERT: I'd like to have a little chat with you if that's all right, Cem. Or would you rather I addressed you formally?

CEM shakes his head.

CEM: Cem's fine.

KOBERT: I'm going to ask you a question or two. You don't have to answer. It's up to you. And if there's anything you want to say –

CEM: Meaning?

KOBERT: Well, I'm going to be writing an assessment for the trial about you.

CEM: Like a school report, or what?

KOBERT: No, an assessment.

CEM: So they can convict me?

KOBERT: It will help the court come to a decision.

CEM nods.

CEM: So if you say I'm mental, they'll dump me with the schizos or something?

KOBERT: It's supposed to help them understand what happened.

CEM: Yeah I got that already.

KOBERT: Good, let's begin.

CEM: What happens if you say I'm not right in the head? What then?

KOBERT: It doesn't work like that.

CEM: ?

KOBERT: I'm not going to write anything about anyone being mentally ill; all I do is describe how I see the person – what I think of them.

CEM: So what's the verdict?

KOBERT: Verdict?

CEM: Are you thinking – he's well aggressive; he's obviously got an anger problem! He must have killed her – you can tell from how he's acting. Antisocial, a crazy bastard, you can tell straight off.

KOBERT: I don't have an opinion yet, and I'm not against you. I'm not judging you – we have to get to know each other first.

CEM nods.

CEM: Time for questions about my childhood, is it?

KOBERT: Oh yes?

CEM: That's what always happens in films. They lie on some sofa and talk about how they were losers as kids – doesn't take much to get them snivelling.

KOBERT: Would you like to lie down?

CEM: I'm just saying what it's like in the movies. I don't know if people do that for real. I haven't met a – what are you?

KOBERT: An assessor.

CEM: Is that a job? Assessor? Aren't you police?

KOBERT: I'm a psychologist.

CEM nods.

So you want to talk about your childhood? Or about your family?

CEM: I just said that's what they do in the movies. You hearing me? Not in the movies now, are we?

KOBERT: No.

CEM: And my family's respectable. You get me? All of them. They've got nothing to do with this. No way.

KOBERT: You've three brothers?

CEM: Yep. So?

KOBERT: Nothing, I was just asking.

CEM: And I had a happy childhood. Nothing to do with it.

KOBERT: Okay.

CEM: Look at my hair.

KOBERT: What about your hair?

CEM: It's falling out. A load comes out whenever I brush it.
Same thing happens if put my hand through it – see?

KOBERT: Yes I can see.

CEM: What's that about then? You're the doctor, why's my
hair falling out?

KOBERT: It happens sometimes. The stress – it won't last. It's a
psychosomatic symptom of stress.

CEM nods.

CEM: So that's what you call it.

KOBERT: Yep. Any other medical problems?

CEM: Problems? You know I've got three brothers, and you
know why I'm here, right?!

KOBERT: Yes.

CEM: So why?

KOBERT: You are under suspicion of having killed a young
woman. Not to mention a second young woman with
serious injuries.

CEM runs his hand through his hair.

CEM: See, it happened again. It's doing my head in.

Silence.

So what've you found out? That my hair's falling out.
That's all.

KOBERT: Rather more than that.

CEM: You been trying to trip me up?

KOBERT: No, we're just talking, I told you that already.

CEM nods.

That'll do for today.

CEM: Hang on a minute –

KOBERT: What is it?

CEM: That's it?

KOBERT: I'll be back tomorrow.

CEM: But that wasn't really talking, was it?

KOBERT: Is there something you want to say?

*CEM gestures a negative, indicating **KOBERT** should leave.*

See you then.

SCENE 2

ULLI.

ULLI: I thought they were electric shocks. Like those things, those shock sticks that you hold in your hand… Those toys. Just like that. Not that I could see anything, I was lying on my stomach; I just felt these shocks in my back. I didn't know I was being stabbed. With a knife. Just shock! Shock! Shock! It did hurt, but…like electric shocks. In my back. Elena was stabbed in front, she knew it was a knife. But maybe it still only feels like electric shocks, not like being stabbed. Like how I think being stabbed would feel. Thought. Now I know of course. When it's from the back. But if it's like that from the front, then maybe it wasn't so bad for her. The pain I mean. If she could see she was being stabbed but it only felt like electric shocks. Maybe then dying didn't hurt too much. She died quickly. I don't know.

There's so much I don't know any more. I can still feel where the knife went in, but there's so much I don't

get. Now they're just stabs. Knife stabs. Whenever
I move I can feel them, and I think about what
happened. Think about something I can't get my head
round. Think about Elena. That's what I wrote to her.
I think about you every minute. When I move, Elena
is there. When I move, like to write her a letter, she's
there. She's always there. When I think about her,
on that day, I can't get it together. That's like electric
shocks, too, in my head.

SCENE 3

SINAN, KOBERT.

SINAN: You know each other by sight, you know who's who.
Even if you've never spoken. Like: do you know
him? Yeah that's so and so, all right, that kind of
thing, that's Cem yeah, he's working at Lubecca's
now – and there's other stuff you know, like how
he's got three brothers. One of them's still little, like
about ten or something, but everyone knew the older
ones, and Cem used to tag along with them. His older
brothers were grown-up and Cem was the quiet one,
the younger brother. You're never that important if
you're younger, 'cause of the older ones, even though
he was two years older than me. If you've got two
older brothers, you're the baby, even though the other
one's even younger, but he doesn't count. So Cem
was always tagging along when they were out, and if
he was on his own, then people were always asking,
where's Hassan and Gülem? The three of them, see?
But that was before Lubecca, where he worked,
Lubecca Limited. From then on he had money, and
he bought himself a BMW and hung out without
them. Then Hassan and Gülem weren't on the scene
any more – they were busy with their own thing. To
begin with, Cem was always on the road, out and
about with the car, taking it for a spin. He used to
give people lifts home. Me, too. I live miles out, in

Brökel, and the last bus goes at ten, so he used to give me a lift if it got late. You can't just go home at ten. So he'd take me with him, to Traxx or wherever, or just riding around, seeing what's what, what's up. You just keep path-crossing all the time and then you kind of become a team, and that's how you end up –

KOBERT: End up what?

SINAN: Being mates, you know?

KOBERT: Because he had a car?

SINAN: Nah, 'cause it was sound. I knew people, where to go and that, you're on the scene, and the next day it's like hey, all right mate? That's just how it works.

KOBERT: Friends.

SINAN: Yeah, something like that.

KOBERT: And what does friendship mean to you?

SINAN: I just told you.

KOBERT: Is Cem your best friend?

SINAN: Look I've just told you how I got to know him and what we kind of did together.

KOBERT: But how do you feel about it?

SINAN: Was okay with me.

KOBERT: Yes, I understood that. But why are you friends with Cem?

SINAN: Look, the kids at school, they're like, you can't talk to them, they're social cases. They get nothing, nada, well excepting one or two maybe. Nothing going on up there. They're trash, you know – they can't even talk in sentences. I reckon the Turkish lot can't even speak Turkish, you get me? They go home, play on the computer 'til their brains are mush. They don't go out, don't do anything, never talk about anything – it's always like, hey mate, you heard of this game? Or two thousand points, level four! They're losers, you get me? I want to go out, see my mates, be seen – I want to do something with my life, you get me?

KOBERT: I do.

SINAN: Cem's like me, he looks after himself, he wants to get on. He's not stupid, he thinks about stuff. He knows where it's at. His brothers too – their house is cool. His mum's nice. His dad's strict – but nice though as well – and you don't just veg out in front of the telly round there. There's no one yelling, no one getting at you, nothing like that. They're my kind of people. I look after myself, and if you hang out with dickheads, you end up getting like them – I know loads like that. In school, I told you, I keep out of it, I've got nothing to do with them, they're dirt. I'm not being arrogant or anything, but they're – you get me?

KOBERT: I understand. So Cem's not like that?

SINAN: Look, I've got nothing against them, they can be like that if they want.

KOBERT: Yes of course.

SINAN: I'm not looking to be better than other people or anything, that's not what I'm about.

KOBERT: It's okay, Sinan.

SINAN: You hearing me?

KOBERT: Yes, of course.

Silence.

SINAN: Yeah so I was mates with Cem.

KOBERT: Was?

SINAN: Is. But I wasn't always out with him. Like the evening he pulled Elena, I wasn't there. I stayed home, 'cause I was going to be out the next day. So I wasn't there. In Traxx. It was his set-up.

KOBERT: The first time he met Elena?

SINAN: I was at home.

KOBERT: Did you know Elena before that?

SINAN: From school, yeah of course, couldn't miss her.

KOBERT: Why?

SINAN: 'Cause she was… Oh shit!

Lighting change, loud music.

SCENE 4

ELENA, CEM.

CEM: Want a drink?

ELENA: Why?

CEM: You've been dancing for ages, must be thirsty.

ELENA: So you're gonna run around buying all the sweaty girls drinks?

CEM: I'm offering you a drink.

ELENA: Awww, listen to him, must be my lucky night.

CEM: Too right it is.

ELENA: And how am I supposed to know you haven't put something in it?

CEM drinks.

You don't imagine I'm gonna have your half-gobbed slobbery coke?

CEM: Then have mine, I've not touched it yet.

ELENA takes the coke, drinks, looks at CEM, CEM drinks as well.

ELENA: So now what?

CEM: What?

ELENA: What's next? Let me guess, you're going to ask my name and then you're going to tell me what a pretty name it is.

CEM: Elena is a pretty name.

ELENA: Oh so you know my name, do you?

CEM: My mate Sinan. From your school.

ELENA: Don't know him.

CEM: But he knows you.

ELENA: Oh that makes me feel really great. So Sinan knows me. And Sinan told you to buy me a coke did he.

CEM: Sinan's not here. I'm here on my own.

ELENA: So now you know me.

CEM: That was the plan.

ELENA: So have you got a name? Or have you forgotten it?

CEM: Cem.

ELENA: Fucking Turkish all over the place can't get away from them.

CEM: Your dad's Turkish, isn't he?

ELENA: But my mum isn't.

Silence.

We done? Nice meeting you, Cem, okay?

CEM: Going for a spin tomorrow. To Cologne.

ELENA: Aren't you lucky.

CEM: Sinan's coming too. That's two places going spare. In my BMW. Morning there, back in the evening.

ELENA: So?

CEM: Cologne's all right. Shops, cafés, funfair…

ELENA: Yeah, I know.

CEM: Wanna come?

ELENA: And what would I want there, with you guys?

CEM: Make a day of it…

ELENA: Drive all the way to Cologne with two guys I've never seen in my life before, you must be fucking joking.

CEM: Bring a mate.

ELENA: Okay, my boyfriend.

CEM: You don't have one.

ELENA: Your friend Sinan know what colour my knickers are, too?

CEM: Bring your mate. We can do something together, or you can do your thing and we'll do ours and we'll meet to come back. I'm going anyway, I've got business. You in?

ELENA: I'll think about it.

CEM: Get away from all this shit, just for a day.

ELENA: I said, I'll think about it.

CEM: Let me know in half an hour, okay?

ELENA: Stop hassling!

CEM: Give me your number and I'll call you before we go.

ELENA: You tell me what time you're leaving and either I'll be there, or I won't.

CEM: Or you ring me.

ELENA: Hello? You deaf or what?

CEM: Okay. We'll be at the Elf petrol station on the B 12, about 11.

ELENA: If I'm not there by quarter past, then I'm not coming. And if I don't come, and we bump into each other again, I don't need you giving me a hard time, okay?

CEM: It was only an offer.

ELENA: Thanks for the coke.

ELENA exits. Lighting change.

SCENE 5

ULLI.

ULLI: She came in and we were laughing 'cause yet again some guy had hit on her, wanted to take her to

114

Cologne, bought her a coke… Happened all the time. Sometimes they even talked to me, you're Elena's friend, aren't you, that kind of thing. You could tell pretty quickly – they'd be hanging around and then they'd ask did we want a drink and we'd let them buy us one, and then you'd have to work out how to get away. Sometimes Elena would start a fight about nothing, she'd suddenly get offended about something and then she'd just say, we're going, stupid wankers. Afterwards we'd piss ourselves laughing. Was that wrong?

I keep asking myself if it was wrong. It was never her that came on to them, even if that's what they all say. She wasn't like that. She wasn't like what they all thought. They all thought, with Elena you can go the whole way, she's up for it. Why did they think that? I'm not saying she was an angel. It's just that she didn't give a toss, and if she didn't give a toss, nor did I. I know she could flip, pretty badly. I've been there. About something really small. She didn't flirt, she never encouraged them, they were just there. But then everyone goes around like she's a slag. They all do… It's just not true. Like bees to the honey pot, I said once, and she said, no, like flies to shit, that's what I am to them, shit.

SCENE 6

KOBERT, CEM.

KOBERT: And women?

CEM: You want to talk about that now?!

KOBERT: Do you?

CEM: Why not. Let's talk about women. What do you want to know, doctor?

KOBERT: How do you feel about women?

CEM: A good woman, like that.

CEM makes a fist and makes the typical aggressive 'phwoar' sign by slapping his hand on his upper arm whilst raising his fist, laughs.

KOBERT: You're a ladies' man?

CEM: You mean, do women like me?

KOBERT: Do they?

CEM: I'll put it this way: I've got a job, so I've got money, right, I've got a car, a BMW 3-series, I know how to talk to women, I take care of myself – I don't hang around with trousers half way down my arse, with zits and trainers and greasy hair and shit. I look after myself, I'm no dirty pikey. No one can say that I'm trash. I've got a good family, I get respect. And it's about having your lines ready, not just in-yer-face.

KOBERT: So how do you talk to women, then?

CEM: You have to be friendly, polite – you have to respect women. Lots of people just don't get it, they piss women off with their talk. Women have to be respected, right?

KOBERT: Yes, absolutely.

CEM: That's how I was brought up – that's the way it's done.

KOBERT: And have you talked to a lot of women?

CEM: I'm a man, aren't I?

KOBERT: Have you ever been in love?

CEM: When I get married I'll be in love.

KOBERT: Do you mind whether your women are German or Turkish?

CEM: I want my women to be beautiful, you get me? Or do you like 'em ugly?

KOBERT: And that's why you chatted up Elena? You saw her and thought, I'll talk to her?

CEM: What do you want to talk about now? You asked me what I think of women, right?

KOBERT: And you respect women.

CEM: And now you're asking me about Elena.

KOBERT: There's a difference?

CEM: Course there's a difference.

KOBERT: In what way?

CEM: She was a slapper. If you want to talk about women, let's talk about women – women you can respect: who could be your girlfriend, who you could marry. It's totally different. I don't want soiled goods. I'm going to marry a nice girl, someone who hasn't been to bed with everyone going. I don't want a girl who's used – Elena was a slapper.

KOBERT: So you don't have to respect her?

CEM: It's just different. It's not what she's looking for either. You can't compare. Why's she out on her own then? I know why she gives me hassle when I talk to her, I know why, 'cause that's what they're like.

KOBERT: They?

CEM: Her sort.

KOBERT: What sort?

CEM: You know what I mean, don't you? Look, you know what you're dealing with, you check it out, don't you? Who'll let you, and who won't. Or what the talk is. About her. Or then what they say about you.

KOBERT: Who?

CEM: The people you hang out with – at home, at your mates'. Look you can't just say it's the same thing. You know what I'm talking about.

KOBERT: Who decides?

CEM: Don't you get it? You gay?

KOBERT: I just want you to explain it to me. You knew who Elena was, Sinan had told you.

CEM: Yes.

KOBERT: And you invited her to go on a trip out of town with you.

CEM: She was mine, and her friend, if she turned up, was for Sinan. No problem.

KOBERT: What would have happened if she'd got together with Sinan?

CEM: Sinan had her friend.

KOBERT: But it wasn't out of the question –

CEM: I did the talking so I get the girl. That's how it's done.

KOBERT: So the girl gets no say in it?

CEM: You really don't get it, do you.

KOBERT: Slappers don't get a say?

CEM: It was me that talked to her. It was me that asked them. They turned up, didn't they? No one was forcing them.

KOBERT: Why are you getting so worked up? I just don't understand the difference between slappers and women.

CEM: Maybe you've only ever met slappers.

SCENE 7

ULLI.

ULLI: She wasn't gonna go. Me neither. She just said that to get rid of him, and because she found it funny imagining him and his mate, with their slicked back hair, standing around like a couple of eejits at the Esso station. Made her laugh.

Then we left, straight away, so he wouldn't come back, and went on to Alcazar. I left before Elena.

About an hour later there was a knock at my window, Elena was there, she'd been in massive trouble for coming home late, and she'd just gone off again and come to mine. She was really pissed off and said let's go to Cologne, let them stew, I want to get away for the day.

My parents went off early the next morning – they were going to a Wild West thing in Dorsten. I'd told them I was going to hang out with Elena. I didn't say anything about the guys.

Was that wrong? I don't know. Elena had everything under control, she knew what was what. And I knew Sinan – he was a bit of a clown – he wasn't the sort to start anything. He just fools around, you could trust him, you know – that everything would be okay, if we went with them. It's a respect thing, you know?

SCENE 8

CEM, SINAN.

SINAN: It's a quarter past, they're not coming.

CEM: Relax will you?

SINAN: Know what I reckon? Wanna hear?

CEM: Like that shirt do you?

SINAN: Don't you? Hugo Boss.

CEM: Wore it specially, did you? Wanna look good for the girls, right?

SINAN: It looks good, yeah.

CEM: So you wore it 'cause you reckoned they'd show, right?

SINAN: If they show.

CEM: Well then.

SINAN: Know what I reckon?

CEM: What?

SINAN: She just said that to get rid of you. Like – you wait there, no mobile, go on, quarter past, and fuck off.

CEM: There you are in your fucking Hugo shirt, pissing yourself you're so wound up – and you're telling me they won't turn up?

SINAN: I'm just saying what's in my mind, okay?

CEM: You reckon I got no technique, that she just thought whatever, stand him up, he's not worth it!? You think I haven't got what it takes to get her to come along? You think I was a total fucking prick? Is that what you think? Do you really think I'm that stupid?

SINAN: Not 'cause of you.

CEM: Don't see anyone else here.

SINAN: 'Cause of her. 'Cause that's what she's like. She's pretty hardcore.

CEM: She's like what she's like, okay? I know what she's like. Hardcore. Whatever. Doesn't bother me. I know what I want. I was there, I spoke to her; it's all going to plan. You reckon you could have pulled it off? Got them along?

SINAN: That's not what I'm saying.

CEM: I've got the car, I planned it, I was friendly to her, told her she could bring her friend – sorted her for you, didn't I? We'll make it nice for them, show them a good time, everyone will be buzzing, okay?

SINAN: Okay.

CEM: Do you know her friend?

SINAN: Yeah, by sight. Nothing special.

CEM: Man, stop bitching. If you get it on, doesn't matter, does it?

SINAN: For sure.

CEM: And that's what it's about. We're gonna have us a good time. Perfect. A perfect day.

SINAN: (*Singing.*) How far does she go?
How far does she go
Tell me baby, you a horny 'ho.

CEM laughs.

Okay – you do your thing, and I'll do mine – just don't give me any hassle. Just don't get in my way today, yeah? Just leave me be for once, you get me?!

SINAN laughs. CEM gives SINAN some money.

CEM: Go get us some crisps and coke and shit, then.

SINAN: Shouldn't we hang on a bit?

CEM: Come on man, if you're not back in five minutes, we'll go without you.

SINAN: Okay, okay.

SINAN exits. CEM lights a cigarette, ELENA and ULLI enter.

ELENA: You still here? It's almost half past.

CEM: Women never show on time.

ELENA: Know all about women, do you?

CEM: Can't you tell?

ELENA: And what would give me that impression?

CEM: I've done a deal for the sunshine, with a couple of clouds so it doesn't get too hot in the car. Not everyone thinks of that. Goes on a trip with a pair of beautiful women and it pisses it with rain. Total shit. Wouldn't happen to me though – you have to think of these things in advance. Sun and a couple of clouds – wasn't cheap. Worth it though, yeah? Make it a bit special.

ULLI: Otherwise we wouldn't be here.

CEM: What's your name?

ULLI: Ulli. Where's Sinan?

121

CEM: Gone to fetch supplies for the journey – everything a woman could want.

ELENA: And you know what that is, do you?

CEM: I reckon. You don't think so?

ELENA: Maybe?

ULLI: I brought some stuff too.

CEM: No need. You girls say what you want, and I'll get it for you.

ELENA: Get us to Cologne, then. Show us a good time!

CEM: Sinan, you wanker! Hurry up, we want to get on the road!

The girls laugh.

SCENE 9

SINAN, KOBERT.

SINAN: It was cool as fuck. One of those moments – you know somehow perfect. You come out of the petrol station, there's Cem standing with the two girls next to the BMW, Saturday morning, sunshine, the day ahead. Even Ulli looked kind of sexy, and she was mine. Superwomen. Elena anyway, the two of them and us, the whole day ahead of us, and everything sorted. I felt kind of proud, you know what I mean?

KOBERT: Of what?

SINAN: That everything was going like we planned, that for once things were like they were supposed to be. Mental, isn't it?

KOBERT: Why? They knew you from school. Why shouldn't they come along?

SINAN: They knew me around, that's all. Everyone knows me but only like – hey, nutter! That kind of thing.

KOBERT: You know a lot of people?

SINAN: Everybody. Good memory for faces – I only need to see somebody once and I've got them stored.

KOBERT: And lots of people know you.

SINAN: I like chatting, you know, like – what's up? where's the party? What's the story? What's going down?

KOBERT: And how do you think people see you?

SINAN: How people rate me, you mean?

KOBERT: Yes.

SINAN: Shit, the nutter's coming, get outta there!

SINAN laughs.

I just like joking around, partying.

KOBERT: You know lots of girls?

SINAN: I told you, I know everyone. But no girlfriend or whatever, nah.

KOBERT: Why not?

SINAN: You'll have to ask the laydeez. They're mad, I'm a stud, init?!

SINAN laughs.

They just don't like chat and that. You know, if you've got money, a car, a job or whatever – or muscles, nice threads, then… But I don't give a toss, you know? I'm on track. Do my apprenticeship, get my own shop, and then back to Turkey – buy me a Mercedes, house, the lot. Then I'll sort the woman thing, I'll line them up, and I'll take my pick.

One for family stuff, kids and the house and that, and one for bed, one who's well up for it. She's gotta be hot for the hardcore stuff. Two women, loads do it, people always talking about it.

KOBERT: You can't have both with your own wife?

SINAN: Sure, she's got to be good in bed too, and pretty – but I don't mean that, I'm talking about something different. It's gonna happen, I know it.

KOBERT: What?

SINAN: I'm going to get somewhere in life. Then I'll be a guy who's respected, then I'll be the boss. So she'll have to be able to look up to me, right?

And I'll make it, no fear. I'm not stupid, okay? In school – okay – but there's more to life –

KOBERT: In Turkey?

SINAN: It's different there.

KOBERT: How do you know?

SINAN: Anyone'll tell you. I'm always saying to my dad why don't we go back? We'd be kings there. But he doesn't want to, he just wants to go on knackering himself. He doesn't realise but he's had it, for real. My mother and sister, they have jobs here and they're like what would we do there? I mean, we're Turkish, aren't we? Who gives a toss if we were born here but it's always 'my job this, my job that'. It's fucked up, you know? My father would get work over there again. Why are they knackering themselves here, when you could be a king over there? It's always no, no, there's no way... There's always a way, if you want it enough. Like when I got back with the coke and crisps: the girls were there. If you want something, you have to have something to offer. You have to go for it.

KOBERT: Do you really believe that what women look for in a man is just money and a car, and that kind of thing?

SINAN: I mean, they turned up, didn't they? They turned up because Cem had got it sorted. It's not about love or whatever, that sort of thing only happens in films. That's why you go to the cinema.

KOBERT: But it didn't work out like it was supposed to, did it?

SINAN: No, course not. Wasn't my fault though. I did what I could.

KOBERT: And what would that be?

SINAN: Making everyone laugh and that. Which I did.

SINAN starts to sing, lighting change.

SCENE 10

CEM, SINAN, ULLI, ELENA. SINAN is singing.

SINAN: Self protection is the name of the game
Cops taking bribes
Take you for a ride
Government drinks wine
What's yours will be mine
He kills she kills
In cities in hills
Murders on the street
Blood is a bitch on heat
Some are killers some are killed, no one is the same
Self protection is the name, the name of the game

SINAN stops singing, ELENA and ULLI clap.

Like it do ya? Gets ya going does it? Sido,[1] Azad,[2] Kool Savas,[3] the whole fucking lot of them can go fuck themselves, I'm number one, I'm better than any of 'em, right?! Right? Right... Am I not the best? I'm asking you! Am I the best? I want to hear a yes. People, I'm not hearing you. The bullet's got your name on it, Sido. I'm on my way up!!

ULLI: You need a mask![4]

ELENA: Put the crisp packet over your head.

The girls try to put the crisp packet over SINAN's head. He wrestles with ULLI.

---

1 Stage name for German rapper, Paul Würdig, born in Berlin.

2 Azad, German rapper, originally from Kurdish part of Iran. Raps in English, Kurdish and German.

3 Kool Savas, German rapper of Turkish descent.

4 Sido uses provocative and aggressive lyrics, and is often seen wearing a silver skull mask. The name 'sido' is an abbreviation for 'super-intelligentes Drogenopfer' (super intelligent drug victim). However, the name originally meant 'Scheiße in Dein Ohr' (Shit into your ear).

SINAN: I'm the business? No? Think I look shit? Shit! Watch that lorry! One dive and I'm roadkill. I'm dead, man!

CEM: You already look like you been run over by a lorry.

SINAN sits down again, next to ULLI, and passes round the crisps and coke.

ULLI: Anything else you can sing? Another one, go on!

SINAN: You hear that, mate? I'm going to sing her a love song so hot she'll cream her knickers, she'll be mad for it! I'm going to sing, Ulli, just you wait, I'm really gonna do it, I've warned you...

ULLI: Go on then, go on!

ELENA: Is there any more coke?

CEM: What do you want? Anything I can get you?

ELENA: Nah, nothing urgent.

SINAN: Okay. Porno hiphop, safe. No fear, I'm singin' in ya ear... Get it on!

SINAN leans over to ULLI and sings quietly into her ear. ULLI giggles.

ELENA: What you looking at?

CEM: I was gonna say something –

ELENA: Spit it out.

CEM: Forgotten. Maybe looking at you will help me remember.

ELENA: You just have a good look then. Shall we get going?

CEM indicates his cigarette.

CEM: Three drags.

ELENA: You can smoke in the car.

CEM: I don't want the car stinking.

ELENA: How long before we get there?

CEM: Twenty minutes, if it's clear.

ELENA: Whereabouts in Cologne are you going?

CEM: Where do you want to go?

ELENA: I thought you had business?

CEM: Did I?

ELENA: Which is why you were going.

CEM: It's sorted. The day's yours.

ELENA looks at him.

ELENA: Sly, eh? And if we hadn't turned up?

CEM: But you did.

ELENA: You're just giving us a lift, okay, we're doing our own thing. Right, Ulli? Leave that dickhead alone! What's the plan?

ULLI: Whatever you're up for.

ELENA: Shopping, coffee, watch the world go by. When are you guys going back? What time shall we meet?

CEM: You need money for shopping, don't you?

ELENA: Not your problem. So what time?

CEM: Dunno.

ELENA: Okay, we'll stay over in Cologne.

CEM: How you gonna do that?

ULLI: An aunt of mine lives here.

ELENA: What do you say to that? Not so clever now, eh? Didn't have business in Cologne after all?

CEM: It'll be a day to remember. Like you've only dreamed of!

ELENA: Let's hear it then.

CEM: Funfair in Deutz.

ELENA: Go on.

CEM: Get something tasty to eat.

ELENA: Go on.

CEM: Take you girls shopping.

ELENA: Go on.

CEM: That's it.

Silence.

ULLI: I think it sounds cool. Elena?

ELENA looks at CEM, he seems a little irritated.

ELENA: You're on.

CEM: Together?

ELENA: If you play your cards right.

CEM: Okay.

ELENA: Scared?

CEM: What of?

ELENA: Right, let's go! Give us a fag, I want to smoke in the car.

CEM gives her a cigarette and lights it, they exit.

SCENE 11

ULLI.

ULLI: One lunch break when we went to the wall where we always smoked, there were these kids from year eight. Elena told them to shift. I don't know if they were ignoring her, or just didn't hear, but they just kept on talking. I wanted to leave it, didn't bother me, but Elena grabbed one of them, pulled her off the wall, and kicked her. Then she went over to the next one and slapped her so hard she fell into the bushes behind the wall. The girl picked herself up and ran off, but when the other one tried get up, Elena kicked her again. Then Elena sat down, lit up, and gave me one. Didn't take long for the teacher on duty to come over with one of them – people started gathering round us, it was really tense. Elena was totally calm though. The teacher had a go at her, like what was she playing at? She just said: this is our wall. No more than that. He started on with 'the playground's for everyone', and she just said: not this wall. The rest of it, maybe, but not here. Afterwards there was a massive fuss and she got hauled up in front of the headmaster, because one of the girls had really got hurt. But Elena didn't care. I wouldn't have minded smoking somewhere else, I didn't give a toss – but she wouldn't give way, she couldn't stand people pissing her off, not respecting her. No way. She'd rather get into trouble – no matter how bad. She never gave in. Never. Not in my experience, anyway. No one sat on the wall any more when we were around.

SCENE 12

CEM, ELENA, SINAN, ULLI.

*Funfair, at a shooting gallery, **SINAN** with a rifle, **ULLI** comes with candy floss for her and **ELENA**, she gives the change to **CEM**.*

SINAN: Is it loaded?

SINAN looks down the barrel of the gun.

Hello! Anyone there?

ULLI: Stop it! It's dangerous.

SINAN: You worried about me? You love me? Is there anybody there?

ELENA: You're starting to bore me, leave it out.

SINAN: Cem, you hear that? They both love me, they don't want me to die…

CEM: Stop pissing around. Shoot, will you.

SINAN: Shoot, I'm gonna shoot. Who shall I shoot? I'm gonna gun you all down. There they are, there! The balloons are everywhere! They're surrounding us, shit!

ULLI: Easy. Calm down.

SINAN: Easy are you? You wanna go down on me? I mean – German it ain't me mother tongue, I'm a Turk, I know fuck.

ELENA: You're boring me...

SINAN: Okay, okay. Three shots get a bear. Like a bear, would you?

ULLI: Just have your go, will you?

SINAN: Okay, I'm taking a shot. For you, I'm doing it for you, baby!

SINAN turns around and shoots at the balloons, and hits three. A moment of astonishment all round.

ULLI: Wow, not bad...

SINAN: What did I say?

SINAN takes a teddy bear from the wall.

What do I get?

ULLI gives him a kiss on the cheek.

ELENA: Nice one, Sinan. Right, where shall we go next?

CEM: My go.

SINAN: Come on, let's go on the dodgems. Can't beat Cem on them, right mate?

CEM: Which one do you want, Elena, choose one!

ELENA: The little dinosaur.

CEM aims and shoots a round, but misses.

Fuck it.

CEM: That was just the warm up. Now for real.

SINAN: Go for it, mate.

CEM shoots again, but only hits one balloon.

CEM: The barrel's bent, it's fucked.

ELENA laughs and briefly musses CEM's hair.

ELENA: Don't get all worked up, I don't want it anyway.

CEM: Shut it for a minute can you guys, gotta focus.

ELENA: You don't need to put on a show for my sake.

ULLI: I'm bored now, can we go?

SINAN: He'll get it, I promise.

> *CEM shoots again, misses.*

CEM: Sinan you fucking dickhead, I told you to shut it.

SINAN: But I was just saying you'll do it!

CEM: No crap from you all right?! Just 'cause not all of us waste our lives shooting shit on playstation – I don't need you mouthing off here, thanks all the same.

SINAN: It was just chance I didn't miss.

ELENA: Don't talk yourself down, you're really good.

ULLI: Can we get going now?

CEM: Will you all shut the fuck up?

ELENA: Sometime this century?

CEM: You wanted me to get you the dinosaur.

ELENA: I don't want anything from you.

> *CEM aims at ELENA.*

CEM: You'll get it, if I want you to.

> *CEM aims, fires, hits two balloons, rips the toy dinosaur off the wall and pushes it into ELENA's hands.*

You wanted it. Now you've got it. When I want something, I get it. That's what I'm like.

> *CEM takes ELENA's head and kisses her on the mouth, she wriggles free.*

All right. Dodgems, anyone?

SINAN: You da man.

CEM: All right, let's go.

> *CEM points at the dinosaur ELENA is holding.*

Cute little thing.

ELENA: Yeah, he can even fly!

*ELENA chucks the dinosaur high into the sky. CEM
exits, followed by SINAN.*

SCENE 13

CEM, KOBERT.

CEM: They had it in for me, no question. There was
something going on, I sussed it. No one fucks around
with me like that.

KOBERT: But you chose to have a go.

CEM: But they forced me to it, the lot of them.

KOBERT: Sinan too?

CEM: He knows I'm short-sighted in my left eye.

KOBERT: He wanted to go on the dodgems with you.

CEM: He was arsing around. Making a fool of himself. That
slapper, too – this is what she did.

CEM musses KOBERT's hair.

You get me?

KOBERT: It could have been meant nicely.

CEM: Like I was a kid, or a dog. Not with me.

KOBERT: How would you have liked her to touch you?

CEM: She doesn't touch me – I touch her.

KOBERT: Is that how you kissed her?

CEM: They wanted to make me look stupid, all of them.
I had to show them who's in charge. Don't you get
that? Don't you know anything? You'd have to be a
fucking idiot not to get it.

KOBERT: Calm down.

CEM: Shit, it makes me really mad, there's no point talking
to you, you just don't get it. I've had enough.

KOBERT: Do you get angry easily?

    Silence.

CEM: So you reckon you got me now, do you?

KOBERT: Why shouldn't you be angry? If three people are ganging up on you?

CEM: Looked that way.

KOBERT: You pointed the gun at her. Were you angry?

CEM: Was just a joke, didn't mean anything. There's no way I could kill someone.

KOBERT: Sometimes I think I could.

CEM: Yeah?

KOBERT: Anyone.

CEM: For real?

KOBERT: If someone was threatening my family, I could kill. Can you imagine that?

CEM: Sure, you've got to defend your family.

KOBERT: So, they provoked you…

CEM: Listen to me a minute. They disrespected me, they had it in for me – same as if they'd attacked me. But that doesn't mean I go and kill someone, okay? I'm not a murderer, get it?

KOBERT: If you say so.

CEM: I am not a murderer. Murder's different. You should stop trying to make assumptions about me – I don't want to be mates with you, you've no idea, you already got a family and that! You're police and you're trying to tell me you could kill someone. We're not talking man to man here, okay? You know nothing about my life! You've no need to defend yourself – no one's fucking with you, okay? So if you tell them I'm violent or keep flipping out, then –

KOBERT: Then? What then?

CEM: You threatening me?

KOBERT: You are threatening me.

CEM: Why would I threaten you? I'm trying to explain you something. I'm stuck in prison here – you can destroy me, but you can't treat me like an arsehole.

KOBERT: That's not what I'm doing.

CEM: I don't get angry easily.

KOBERT: I didn't say you did.

CEM: I was just saying things weren't going well, that's all. Everything that happened was because of what they did, not 'cause of me. Everything, get it? Everything!

SCENE 14

ULLI.

ULLI: I thought that was going to be it. I don't know why Elena stayed. Normally, if something like that happened, either she'd just leave or she'd make real trouble. She was really angry, I know she was, but she just said, let's go shopping. You could already see what Cem was like, had to be boss, the coolest, all that crap. Sinan tried to make it better, fooling around and everything, I felt really sorry for him – he was really trying. Cem slouched along behind us. Elena was looking in shop windows, putting up a front like he hadn't got to her – and at some point I thought, okay, perhaps I'm being oversensitive, perhaps it wasn't anything much. If Elena's got over it, maybe it's not important. And I liked Sinan, he's a nutter, but he was fun. So in Ehren Street we went into this clothes shop.

Music, lighting change.

SCENE 15

CEM, SINAN, ULLI.

ULLI holds a dress up against herself.

ULLI: What do you think of this?

SINAN: Dunno. What do you think, Cem?

CEM: Dunno.

SINAN: I dunno either.

ULLI: You have to imagine it with other shoes.

SINAN: What have shoes got to do with it?

ULLI: You've no idea, have you?

> *ELENA comes out of the changing room, she is wearing a light summer dress, high heels, and her hair is down. She walks round the room, like a model, stops briefly, right up close to CEM, looks at him for a moment, and then goes over to SINAN.*

ELENA: Shut your mouth, it's getting drafty.

> *She goes over to ULLI.*

What do you think? Does it suit me? Do you like it?

ULLI: It's a bit see-through.

> *ELENA looks down at herself.*

ELENA: It'll look well sexy with a tan.

> *To SINAN and CEM.*

Bored, are we? That's what it's like when women go shopping. Want to wait outside? Why don't you get yourselves a kebab?

CEM: Nah, it's all right.

ELENA: Turned out well, hasn't it? You've really done it, boys, a fantastic day. But you don't have to buy me the dress, Cem, leave your money where it is. If I need something, I'll get it myself.

CEM: Shall I buy you the dress?

ELENA: You don't have to, put it away.

ELENA goes back into the changing room.

SCENE 16

SINAN, CEM.

SINAN: She was coming on to him, she had this dress on and you could see everything – her tits, her knickers, it was like she wasn't wearing anything. She went over to Cem and it was well turning him on. That's what she wanted, like porn she was so hot. She was gagging for him, no question.

KOBERT: I thought you guys weren't getting on.

SINAN: Who said that?

KOBERT: After the shooting fiasco.

SINAN: That wasn't anything, everything was fine.

Silence.

You don't believe me? What you thinking it was like then? Just because Cem missed a few times? No one gave a toss, she'd even touched him already, run her hand through his hair. It all came from her, she started it.

KOBERT: Cem wasn't annoyed then?

SINAN: We were all doing fine.

KOBERT: You didn't force him to have a go in the shooting gallery?

SINAN: What? Us?

KOBERT: All right all right.

SINAN: Is that what Cem told you?

KOBERT: So she provoked him?

SINAN: What did Cem say? What's he been saying about me?

KOBERT: Nothing.

SINAN: I can't remember the exact details anymore.

KOBERT: So Cem was in a good mood?

SINAN: What's he been saying?

KOBERT: Nothing, he just remembers it differently, that's all.

SCENE 17

ULLI.

ULLI: Once we had this trainee teacher, a right arsehole. He had a go at Elena the first time he took us in class because she was late or something. Elena didn't say anything, she just let him go on shouting. After that though, she always came to class in the sexiest clothes she had, skirt right up to her bum, loads of cleavage. She just sat there in his classes and stared at him. He'd get really red, could hardly look at her, but she'd just stare right at him, the whole time, and she'd walk past him really close when she left class. He never said anything to her again, but you could tell she was getting to him. She just saw it through, ice-cool, didn't care what the others were saying about her. When she got all dressed up, she was untouchable. That's how I want to remember her, in that dress, untouchable.

SCENE 18

CEM, KOBERT.

KOBERT: So, you don't feel like talking today.

CEM shakes his head.

I don't want to force you.

CEM: It's not going to make any difference. Nothing was like what I told you.

KOBERT: So how was it?

CEM: I don't know any more.

KOBERT: You tired?

CEM: Yes.

Silence.

What's wrong with me? You're the shrink. What's wrong with me?

KOBERT: I don't know. Talk to me.

CEM: I keep having stupid dreams.

KOBERT: What do you dream about?

CEM: I dream about brightly lit spaces, neon lights, like in a warehouse, fat neon strip lighting, and I'm small, so small, and I can't get out, I can barely reach the door handle.

KOBERT: In these dreams, are you alone?

CEM: The girl's there. Huge. She stands in front of me and looks down at me.

KOBERT: Does she say anything?

CEM: She just looks at me.

KOBERT: And how does she seem to you? Angry? Friendly?

CEM: I can't tell, it's too far away, I'm much too small, she's just somewhere up there. She is grinning, and I know she's got total contempt for me. There's nothing I can give her, she's doing fine on her own, just fine.

Silence.

I'm not a failure, am I? Kobert?

Silence.

Why aren't you saying anything?

KOBERT: Because I don't believe you.

CEM: I feel like shit.

KOBERT: Maybe you do.

CEM *looks at* **KOBERT**.

CEM: You don't believe me?

KOBERT: No, I don't believe you.

> *Silence.*

CEM: Not so stupid after all.

KOBERT: No, funnily enough, I'm not.

CEM: You've listened to a lot of shit for someone who's not stupid.

KOBERT: That's my job.

CEM: Crap job, eh?

KOBERT: There's always some truth in it somewhere.

CEM: Not with me. About the funfair, and them taking the piss, that was total crap, doesn't matter to me if the slapper lips off all the time, not my problem. Did you really believe I took her seriously? Not for a minute. She was stringing me along, right from the beginning.

KOBERT: So everything was okay?

CEM: Yeah it was.

KOBERT: All fine?

CEM: Yes.

> *KOBERT gets up, takes a few steps.*

You got a problem?

KOBERT: I'm going to ask to be released from this case – someone else can take my place. I've can't be bothered to waste my time with you any longer. Your games are starting to get on my nerves; I'm fed up with it.

CEM: But you have to.

KOBERT: I don't have to.

CEM: It's your job.

KOBERT: You'll be told when the new assessor arrives. Bye.

CEM: Wait a minute.

KOBERT: What for? Are you planning on telling me that Elena gave herself thirty stab wounds? And that Ulli simply danced into the path of a knife because she was a slapper too?

CEM: Fucking shit, I don't know either how it could have happened, I've got no idea. It was self-defence.

KOBERT: I'm not listening to this crap any more.

CEM: I didn't mean it to happen.

KOBERT: Bye!

CEM: You can't just leave!

KOBERT: For days now I've been listening to some cock-and-bull story about a fabulous day out, and somehow I can't quite get my head round what it's got to do with the fact that one girl died and another was left for dead.

CEM: I can't get my head round it either.

KOBERT: But you killed her, didn't you?

CEM: Yes, but what else was I supposed to do?

SCENE 19

CEM, SINAN, ELENA, ULLI.

ELENA: Okay, where now?

SINAN: Do you want to look around a bit more?

ELENA: I've got everything I need. You need anything?

CEM: No.

ELENA: You want anything, Ulli?

ULLI: Didn't see anything.

ELENA: Try this.

ELENA fetches a T-shirt from her bag and gives it to ULLI.

SINAN: Cool.

ULLI holds the T-shirt up against herself.

ELENA: My dress was shit-hot. You liked it?

CEM: It was okay.

ELENA: It wasn't just okay. It was fantastic.

CEM: Okay, it was fantastic.

ELENA: Had to have it.

CEM: If you say so?

ELENA: That dress couldn't resist me, jumped right into my bag – and the shoes didn't want to be left behind, either.

ELENA gets the summer dress and the shoes out of her bag.

Don't get jealous now, I got something for you too.

She fetches a pair of boxer shorts out of her bag and gives them to CEM.

Will it all fit in there?

CEM doesn't respond.

Come on, don't get worked up, it was just a little present. It's not a thong, it's a pair of boxers, okay?

SINAN: Cem, man, it was nice of her.

CEM: I don't need boxers. Got plenty.

ELENA: How am I supposed to know that.

She throws the boxer shorts at SINAN.

Here, Sinan, you have them.

SINAN: Cheers. What about you two?

ELENA: Do we wear underwear, Ulli?

ULLI: Sometimes.

ELENA: Do we have enough underwear, Ulli?

ULLI: Never.

ELENA: Should do something about that. Got the balls?

SINAN: To nick stuff for you?

ELENA: (*To CEM.*) Balls dropped yet, kid?

SINAN: You up for it, mate?

CEM: You do it if you want.

SINAN: Don't be chicken.

CEM: It's kids' games.

ELENA: A g-string for me, size eight, what colour do you reckon?

ULLI: To go with the dress? Light pink.

SINAN: And you?

ULLI: Same for me but in size ten, and black.

> *CEM gets a fifty euro note out of his trouser pocket.*

CEM: Will that do?

SINAN: Can't be that hard.

ULLI: Buying things is no fun.

ELENA: But if he wants to?

SINAN: Can we watch while you try them on?

ELENA: Porno hiphop, is it? Do you have any hair on your balls yet? Cem, need a receipt for when you get home?

ULLI: That's mean, Elena.

ELENA: He knows what I mean.

> *The girls exit.*

SCENE 20

SINAN, KOBERT.

SINAN: I heard Cem had a breakdown?

KOBERT: Cem?

SINAN: Yeah, kind of all done in.

KOBERT: Who's saying that?

SINAN: Just heard it around, not surprised.

KOBERT: Why?

SINAN: He's that type.

KOBERT: Doesn't sound very friendly.

SINAN: I never said we were friends.

KOBERT: No?

SINAN: Wouldn't surprise me, if he talked shit about me.

KOBERT: Why?

SINAN: Because he's got no grip. All the things that went well, that was 'cause of me – the bad stuff, that was him. Sounds harsh, but that's how it was.

KOBERT: So you've been lying up to now?

SINAN: No. But I was too nice. Shouldn't of been. Friends just cause problems. I did my best, but he just didn't get it. Without him everything would have been okay, but he's just little Cem, you know, one of those types who can't get it together. Just so you know, if he tries to tell you anything. You can't believe what he says.

KOBERT: But I'm supposed to believe you?

SINAN: I didn't drop him in it. I had every reason to.

KOBERT: Why?

SINAN: He fucked up.

KOBERT: Does that matter, if you're friends?

SINAN: He's not my friend.

SCENE 21

CEM, SINAN.

CEM: What was that all about? All that pissing around, showing off to them! What is it you want? What? You planning to screw them both? You got it in for me? What's going on?

SINAN: I'm just fooling.

CEM: We had an arrangement. You can fuck off, too – get yourself home on your own – and don't come near me again! I've had it up to here Sinan – up to here!

SINAN: I don't get you!

CEM: Sucking up to them, making a right dick of yourself. That what you call fooling?

SINAN: I don't understand what's going on here.

CEM: You knew the score. This is my game, not yours. Some fucking mate you are! Oh yes we'll nick panties for you, you're so cool, anything else can I do for you? You're not going to make a fool of me, not you! Got it all planned out with them, have you?

SINAN: Everything I've done, it's just to get you to...

CEM: To what? What? They treat me like dirt. Who do they think I am? Some bastard?

SINAN: Then have a go at them, not at me.

CEM: It's you who's sucking up to them.

SINAN: I talk to them like you talk to slappers. I don't give a fuck about them.

CEM: And I don't know how to talk to a slapper, that it?

SINAN: We're a team, and they're just slappers, right? I already warned you, I told you she was hardcore, she's a nutter, she's just dirt.

CEM: I'm going to screw her, and then I'm going to tell her to fuck right off. I'm not leaving it like this!

SINAN: You do that.

CEM: I will, too.

SINAN: Okay.

CEM: Don't you believe me?

SINAN: All you've got to do is shoot the goal home, I'll do the rest.

CEM: You doubting me?

SINAN: You're the boss.

CEM: I already fucked her once. Yesterday. And now she's behaving like a total nutter. She's mine, okay? Now she's behaving like nothing happened.

SINAN: Congratulations!

CEM: Don't you believe me?

SINAN: Why didn't you tell me before?

CEM: Nothing to do with you.

ELENA and ULLI enter running, they are out of breath.

ULLI: That was really close.

ELENA pulls the fifty euro note out of her purse.

ELENA: Didn't need this. I'll treat you guys to the cinema later, okay?

CEM: Okay.

ELENA: Got your cool back?

CEM: Everything's fine, Elena. Isn't it mate? Sorted?

SINAN: Sorted.

ULLI: Cinemaxx?

CEM: Whatever.

They exit.

SCENE 22

ULLI.

ULLI: I don't know what they'd been talking about, but Sinan had gone all quiet, like someone had pulled the plug on him. Cem was friendly: he'd stopped whinging and was being charming again, like he'd

been at the beginning. He fetched us popcorn and
drinks: everything was cool. The cinema was nearly
empty – we sat in the best seats, me and Sinan
together, with Elena and Cem in the row in front.
Sinan still wasn't saying much, but Elena and Cem
were talking quietly. I was thinking that she'd want to
scratch his eyes out, he'd been being such a wanker.
I couldn't get my head round the fact they were
talking. I was sitting there, thinking I just didn't have
a clue about love, about how relationships work and
how people meet and get together and why it works
out sometimes and not others. Then it got dark for the
adverts, but before the film even started, Cem and
Elena got up and left. Elena said they'd meet us after
the film. I sat there in the cinema, in Cologne, with
this boy I didn't know at all, and I couldn't get my
head round anything any more. I felt so totally alone,
totally clueless. I hadn't wanted any of it, and now
I was sitting there, and Elena was outside with this
nutter doing God knows what. Then I snuggled up to
Sinan a bit, I mean he was nice – but even that was
weird, not much happened. All I could think about
was how I wanted to go home, and I was beginning
to think I needed a bit of a break from Elena. I'd had
enough by then, and I was really looking forward to
seeing my mum and dad. When we came out after
the film, Cem and Elena were in a really foul mood.
Something must have gone badly wrong, and that
pissed me off, too, all of it did. I just wanted to get
home, I just wanted it all to be over.

SCENE 23

CEM, KOBERT.

CEM: Can you tell them I'm mental?

KOBERT: Why would I do that?

CEM: Because I am. What I did – no one does that, you'd have to be mental. It's crazy.

KOBERT: Is what you're trying to say, that you weren't responsible for your actions when you committed the crime?

CEM: Can you write something like that?

KOBERT: Why? Do you expect to get a lesser sentence? If you are registered with a psychological disorder, you'll just be put in a clinic, it won't change anything.

CEM: Doesn't matter to me. I'm dead already.

KOBERT: What's that supposed to mean?

CEM: When I get out, one of them'll get me.

KOBERT: Is that why you want to be put in a clinic?

CEM: They'll get me there, too. They'll catch up with me one day. But it doesn't matter.

Silence.

KOBERT: So what does?

CEM: If you say I'm mental, there won't be a trial, right?

KOBERT: Are you scared of the trial?

CEM: Okay – 'It was me', sorted, off to the loony bin yeah, no trouble. Then there'll be no need for anyone nosing around any more.

KOBERT: What are you frightened of?

CEM: Don't believe Sinan, he's lying.

KOBERT: And you? Are you lying too?

CEM: Not any more.

KOBERT: You told Sinan you slept with Elena.

CEM: I did, too.

KOBERT: In the park?

CEM: No, the night before.

Silence.

KOBERT: I'm sorry but I don't believe you.

CEM: Look, that night – after they left the party, they went to Alcazar – and I followed them there in the car. At some point Elena went home. Then I just drove around for a bit, I didn't feel like going home yet. Then I saw Elena on the street, she was trying to hitch a lift, so I picked her up. She was done in, there'd been stress at home and she was going round to her friend's. First though she wanted to drive about for a bit. So I give the car a run, two hundred kilometres an hour, music full volume, window open, out to the reservoir, break for a fag – I don't let people smoke in my car. And that's when it happened...

KOBERT: Whose idea was it?

CEM: Afterwards she said maybe she'd come along, didn't say much else. I dropped her off at her friend's. And then that.

KOBERT: What?

CEM: How it went afterwards. I couldn't get my head round it.

Silence.

KOBERT: Were you in love with her?

CEM: It wasn't like that – I hardly knew her, or her me.

KOBERT: Why didn't you tell Sinan?

CEM: Sinan can't keep his mouth shut. That kind of thing I sort by myself. That's why we left the cinema.

SCENE 24

CEM, ELENA.

CEM: Nothing's over, nothing.

ELENA: There never was anything.

CEM: What about yesterday?

ELENA: Doesn't count, I was feeling lousy. A mistake. It didn't happen, okay?

CEM: I'm not a mistake, though.

ELENA: I shouldn't have come today, pointless, a stupid idea.

CEM: But you're here now.

ELENA: So? We'll just have to go back again.

CEM: Fuck around with me the whole day, and then dump me – no way. No one fucks around with me like that.

ELENA: See? That's exactly what's been doing my head in all day.

CEM: I do your head in, do I?

ELENA: Just chill out, will you, it didn't work out, sorry, okay?

CEM: I fucked you, right? So.

ELENA: So what?

CEM: Like yesterday, like today.

ELENA: Get your hands off of me. We're talking, right? Man, I thought you'd cheered up, what's your problem?

CEM: It's you that's got a problem.

ELENA: So what's that, then?

CEM: You act like a whore.

ELENA: Man, why is it you can't just say to a guy that you don't want to? That you're not up for it?

CEM: Bit late for that.

ELENA: You got rights over me or something? You haven't bought me, okay?

CEM: You came along. You came on to me.

ELENA: Oh yeah?

CEM: I'll give you another twenty, we'll fuck and then we're done.

ELENA: That's your plan is it? You need that to feel like a man?

CEM gets out a banknote, shows it to her.

You really need it that much?

CEM: I've got a right.

ELENA looks at him.

ELENA: Go on then, get it out.

CEM undoes his flies. ELENA looks at him.

CEM: Come on then.

ELENA: You know what? Sometimes even whores don't feel like it. Let's go get the others.

ELENA exits.

SCENE 25

SINAN, KOBERT.

SINAN: When we came out of the cinema, the other two were waiting for us. The mood was totally shit. Cem wasn't speaking and Elena wanted to go straight home. I thought, okay he did what he wanted, fucked her in the park and told her where she could get off. I thought I might still be in with a chance with Ulli, but Elena had a go at me, and Ulli wouldn't even look at me. I was well pissed off, I was thinking, was that it? Just a bit of a snog in the cinema? They'd had their thing, and I could see where I stood. I was pissed off, really pissed off. Elena and Ulli decided they wanted to go to Traxx later and I could see I wasn't part of the plan. Cem didn't say a thing to me, so we just got in the car. We stopped at a petrol station on the way out of town, and that's when it all kicked off.

CEM, ULLI, ELENA

ELENA: Bring us a coke, will you?

CEM doesn't respond.

Hello!? I said can you get me a coke?

CEM: Kiss my arse.

ELENA: What?

CEM: You're getting nothing else from me, nothing, you can fuck off! Now! – I'd give you a hand, but I wouldn't wanna get it dirty.

ELENA: Have you totally lost it?

CEM: Fuck off, both of you, I don't want your dirt in my car, you can both fuck off, you hearing me? Need help?

ULLI: Come on, Elena, we can go to my aunt's, let's go.

ELENA: I'm not going anywhere while this idiot's insulting me, no way.

CEM: You got a hearing problem? You're not coming in my car any more! Dirty bitches.

SINAN: That's when I realised that something must have gone badly wrong between them. But it wasn't my problem, and I still thought I might be able to get somewhere with Ulli.

SINAN talks up to CEM in the scene.

SINAN: What you doing? Come on mate, let them come with us, what the hell happened?

CEM: You should have seen what she was like just now, just because I won't let her near me, for real, I wouldn't even get my finger dirty with someone like that. I've had enough today, now I know what a whore she is, and now she's getting bitchy with me, because I'm too good for her.

ELENA: What are you trying to say?

CEM: Shut your mouth when a man's talking. I'm done with you.

ELENA: Oh yes? I wouldn't be so sure about that.

CEM: So why's that?

ULLI: Then she started talking to Cem in Turkish. I don't know what she said, but he suddenly shut up and we got back in the car. He stopped whinging – somehow

151

she'd managed to put a stopper in it. I tried to work
out what was going on, but I couldn't. She sat in the
front next to Cem, both of them arguing the whole
time – you could see she had him by the balls. Sinan
had totally shut up – he was listening to what they
were saying. I felt shit scared – too scared even to ask
Elena what was going on. It must have been because
of me that they suddenly started speaking Turkish. I
didn't know if she was getting us out of something,
or into something, or if she'd still got things under
control. I'd never seen her so angry, she was electric.
If I'd touched her, I'd have got an electric shock.
So much stupid stuff going round in my head, like
please, please let us have a breakdown, a traffic jam,
anything, doesn't matter where, doesn't matter how
much trouble we get into at home, just please let it be
over. Cem was smoking, he was shaking, and I was
thinking that if he was smoking in the car he must be
in a pretty bad way, you notice things like that. I was
really alert, I was thinking, how do I get out of here,
when the car stops, why is there only two doors, it's
a trap, I just kept thinking these things, all that kind
of shit.

KOBERT: What was going on?

CEM: She'd had it in for me, right from the beginning. Had
it all planned.

KOBERT: Planned? What do you mean when you say the only
thing you could do was to kill her?

ELENA: What if I'm pregnant? What'd you do then? What'd
you do if you had to marry a 'whore'? Eh? How d'you
like that? A kid with a whore? With someone you
don't wanna be seen with, someone who's not good
enough for you? A dirty whore, what then? Eh? Not
so cool now, eh? You gonna carry on spreading lies
about me? Who's gonna be pointing the finger now?!
Don't fancy introducing me to your parents? How
about your brothers? Well? Quick, fuck the slapper,

'cause you're so fly, and then spread shit about me. Serve you right, superman, you'd be finished! Now you're gonna have to think about how you talk to me, you're stuck with me now, and I'm not listening any more to a thing you say, not a thing. I know plenty like you, I know what you all say about me, and I've had enough. You're gonna have to face up to it. So now what you gonna do?

KOBERT: You believed her?

CEM: I'd have lost face, I'd have lost respect, all of us would. I couldn't do that to my family. She wanted to destroy my whole life, my plans, my future, my honour, all respect. I'd have been dissed by all the guys, scorned, I wouldn't have been able to look anyone in the eye. She'd already planned to trap me, she was trying to get me, all along. No way can you trust women like that.

KOBERT: Is that what you really believed?

CEM: She had it in for me. Why would she have done it otherwise?

KOBERT: You didn't think it could be to do with how you were treating her?

CEM: I treated her like she deserved! You're not getting it, are you?

SINAN: I knew she was lying. No woman knows the next day if she's pregnant. But I thought, serve him right to stew in it for a bit, for once. He'd spoilt my day, done my head in – it was his turn for once to get it in the neck. And man did he get it! But I didn't know how far he'd go. By the time he pulled up, she'd stopped going on about the pregnancy thing, she was just swearing at him, really going for him. He must have hurt her bad, she was that upset.

ELENA: Well? Not mouthing off so much now, are we? And no more 'whore' or 'slapper' when you talk to me, you get me? And you'll apologise for everything, okay, and tell people what a load of crap you've been saying about me – or I'll start telling, and then you'll really've had it, okay?

*CEM jumps up, pulls a knife and goes for **ELENA**. He stabs her, she falls to the ground, and he carries on stabbing her as she lies there. **ULLI** shies away, buries her face in her hands. **CEM** leaves **ELENA** and stands over **ULLI**, holding the knife.*

KOBERT: Why didn't you try to stop him?

SINAN: It was all going too fast.

CEM: She's got to go, too.

SINAN: He stabbed the other one, as well.

CEM: Don't lie!

KOBERT: She was stabbed from more than one direction. Two people stabbed her.

SINAN: I stabbed her once, so that he'd think she was dead. I wanted to protect her.

KOBERT: There were several stab wounds.

SINAN: Maybe I stabbed her a couple of times.

KOBERT: Why was that? When you'd had nothing to do with it?

SINAN: Didn't think about it.

KOBERT: Because Cem's your friend?

SINAN: He's not my friend.

KOBERT: Because you were annoyed with Ulli?

SINAN: It wasn't that.

KOBERT: Were you scared Cem would attack you?

SINAN: No.

KOBERT: So there's no reason then for you to have stabbed Ulli, not one.

SINAN: But she was a witness.

KOBERT: Like you were, too.

SINAN: I was hanging out with Cem. She was a witness.

KOBERT: So?

SINAN: Witnesses have to be got rid of.

KOBERT: That's what you thought?

SINAN: You don't have to think about it. There wasn't time for that. It was a matter of respect.

CEM: She's got to go, too!

SINAN jumps up, runs across the stage, pushes ULLI to the ground, takes a knife and stabs ULLI. He leaves her, and CEM stabs her another couple of times. Silence.

CEM: Let's get out of here.

SINAN and CEM quickly exit.

ULLI: I pretended I was dead. After the two of them had gone, I searched for Elena. By the time I found her, she was no longer alive. I lay down next to her and wanted to die too. But I didn't. So I crawled to the road. So much pain. I just was thinking, please God, take me away from all this.

End.

Biographies

JONAS HASSEN KHEMIRI

Jonas Hassen Khemiri, born in 1978, has a Tunisian father and a Swedish mother. His celebrated debut *Ett öga rött/One Eye Red* was published in 2003 selling over 200,000 copies in Sweden. For *Ett öga rött/One Eye Red* Hassen Khemiri received the Borås Tidning award for best literary debut. In 2007 the film based on *Ett öga rött/One Eye Red* opened in Sweden.

Jonas Hassen Khemiri's second novel, *Montecore*, was published in 2006 and was awarded the P O Enquist Prize. *Montecore* was nominated for the August literary award and also received Sveriges Radio's Romanpris award for best novel of 2007.

Jonas Hassen Khemiri's first play *Invasion!* was written for The Stockholm City Theatre. His drama debut also opened the doors for Khemiri to participate at the Royal Court's International Residency in London.

JOËL POMMERAT

Joël Pommerat was born in Roanne in 1963. As both author and director he founded the Louis Brouillard company in 1990, with which he created several pieces including *Pôles* (1995); *Treize étroites têtes* (1997); *Mon ami* (2001); *Qu'est-ce qu'on a fait?* (2003); *Au Monde* (2004); *Le Petit Chaperon Rouge, D'Une Seule Main* (2005); and *Les Marchands* (2006). The Louis Brouillard company has been in residence at the Theatre Bretigny since 1997 and, beginning in 2007, at the Théâtre des Bouffes du Nord for a period of three years. He is published in France by Actes Sud-Papiers.

LUTZ HÜBNER

Lutz Hübner was born at Heilbronn in 1964. After studying German, Philosophy, and Sociology at Münster University he trained as an actor at the Saarbrücken Staatliche Hochschule. There followed engagements as an actor and director in Saarbrücken, Aachen, Neuss, and Magdeburg. Since 1996 Lutz Hübner has worked as a freelance author and director. His plays invclude *Scratch!* (Schauspielhaus Düsseldorf, 2003); *Nellie Goodbye* (Theater Hagen, 2003); *Dramoletti* (theater rampe, Stuttgart, 2003); *Bankenstück* (Maxim Gorki Theater, Berlin, 2004); *Der Machinist* (Staatstheater Braunschweig, 2004); *Hotel Paraiso* (Staatstheater Hannover, 2004); *Leben des Zacarias* (Maxim Gorki Theater, Berlin, 2005). He lives in Berlin.

FRANK PERRY

Frank Perry is a writer and translator living in London who has made a speciality of introducing contemporary Swedish drama to English-speaking audiences throughout the world. He is also known for his translations of modern Swedish poetry and prose together with fiction and plays for children and young people. In 2004 he was awarded the Swedish Academy prize for services to Swedish culture.

ZOË SVENDSEN

Zoë Svendsen is a theatre maker, dividing her time between translation, directing, and research. Her translations include plays by Peter Turrini (also for Theatre Café), Ödön von Horváth (for a translation residency at the National Theatre Studio), Lukas Bärfuss and Heinrich von Kleist. She is currently directing a retelling of Brecht's short story, *Four Men and a Poker Game*, produced in association with Northern Stage.

NIGEL GEARING

Nigel Gearing's previous English adaptations for theatre, film and radio include Molière's *Don Juan*, Azama's *Crossfire*, Sartre's *Roads To Freedom*, Desplechin's *Esther Khan*, Chéreau's *Intimacy* and Alain-Fournier's *Le Grand Meaulnes*. His French adaptations include Marlowe's *Edward II* and Webster's *The Duchess of Malfi*.

Theatre Café 2004

I LOVE THIS COUNTRY / AUSTRIA
   by Peter Turrini translated by Zoë Svendsen (translation commissioned by Company of Angels)

THE DREAMED LIFE OF NORA SCHAHRAZADE / SWEDEN
   by Mia Törnqvist translated by May Brit Akerholt

TIME OF DARKNESS / SWEDEN
   by Henning Mankell translated by Ann Henning Jocelyn

THE LETTER / CROATIA
   by Aleksander Miljkovic translated by Aleksander Miljkovic

MOTHER AFRICA / HOLLAND
   by Ad de Bont translated by Rina Vergano (translation commissioned by Company of Angels)

MAUSOLEUM / HUNGARY
   by Lajos Parti-Nagy translated by John Batki

ENCROACHMENT / CZECH REPUBLIC
   by Iva Volankova translated by David Nykl

TRUCKSTOP / HOLLAND
   By Lot Vekemans translated by Paul Gilling

RAMBO 7 / ICELAND
   by Jon Alti Jonasson translated by Jon Alti Jonasson

THE HEART OF A BOXER / GERMANY
   by Lutz Hübner translated by Penny Black (translation commissioned by Company of Angels)

MOBILE HORROR / FINLAND
   by Juha Jokela translated by David Hackston

THE WILD CHILDREN OF THE BLUE PLANET / ICELAND
   by Andri Snær Magnason translated by Andri Snær Magnason and Julian Meldon D'Arcy

Theatre Café 2007

BATS / PORTUGAL
by Jaime Rocha translated by Alice de Sousa (translation commissioned by Company of Angels)

BLOWING / HOLLAND
by Jeroen van den Berg translated by Rina Vergano

COLÕRS / ROMANIA
by Peca Stefan

DO YOU LIKE PORN? / SWEDEN
by Klas Abrahamsson translated by Gabriella Berggren

THE REAL ELVIS / ESTONIA
by Urmas Vadi translated by Liina Unt

HELVER'S NIGHT / POLAND
by Ingmar Villqist translated by Jacek Laskowski

IN MEMORIAM / BELGIUM
by Hanneke Paauwe translated by Rina Vergano (translation commissioned by Company of Angels)

INVASION! / SWEDEN
by Jonas Hassen Khemiri translated by Frank Perry (translation commissioned by Company of Angels)

RESPECT / GERMANY
by Lutz Hübner translated by Zoë Svendsen (translation commissioned by Company of Angels)

SO YOUNG, SO BLONDE, SO TOTALLY CONFUSED / BELGIUM
by Gerda Dendooven translated by Rina Vergano (translation commissioned by Company of Angels)

THIS CHILD / FRANCE
by Joël Pommerat translated by Nigel Gearing (translation commissioned by Company of Angels)

Theatre Café 2008

SENSE / GERMANY

by Anja Hilling translated by Logan Kennedy and Leonhard Unglaub

NIGHTBLIND / SWITZERLAND

by Darja Stocker translated by Philip Thorne (translation commissioned by Company of Angels)

BULGER / BELGIUM

by Klaas Tindemans translated by Gregory Ball

SANDHOLM / DENMARK

by Anna Bro translated by Mia Theil Have and Max Webster (translation commissioned by Company of Angels)

HEADCASE / HOLLAND

by Esther Gerritsen translated by Rina Vergano (translation commissioned by Company of Angels)